THE END OF THE RICH COUNTRY

Why Life Feels Harder Than It Should — and How Britain Drifted Here

James L. Barton

This book is a work of non-fiction. It reflects the author's interpretation of economic and social trends and is intended for general informational purposes only. It does not constitute financial, legal, or investment advice.

The author has made every effort to ensure the accuracy of information presented at the time of publication. However, economic conditions, policies, and data may change, and no responsibility is accepted for errors or omissions.

First published in the United Kingdom in 2025.

For those who sensed something had shifted

long before anyone named it.

"The illusion of permanence is the most dangerous illusion of all." — Harold Macmillan

Contents

Introduction The Feeling No One Can Quite Explain

You're not imagining it. The country has changed.

Most people don't say that out loud, at least not in company. It sounds dramatic, or nostalgic, or like something you mutter after a bad commute. So the thought usually stays half-formed, filed away under "one of those things". Life just feels harder than it should.

Not desperate. Not catastrophic. Just heavier.

You did what you were supposed to do. You worked, you paid your taxes, you tried to be sensible. You didn't expect luxury, just a degree of ease — that steady sense that effort translated into progress, that problems were solvable, that the system broadly worked if you played by the rules. On paper, things are still fine. And yet money doesn't stretch the way it once did. Public services feel thinner. Everything costs more time, more energy, more admin. Even small problems seem to require persistence, patience, and a low tolerance for frustration.

The strange part is that you're constantly told this shouldn't be happening. Britain is still described as a rich country. A major economy. A global financial centre. A serious player. A place that has weathered worse and always bounced back. We still talk about ourselves using the language of strength, resilience, and quiet superiority.

So when daily life feels tighter, slower, and more brittle, the instinctive response is to turn the criticism inward.

Maybe it's just me.

Maybe I'm misremembering.

Maybe this is just how adulthood feels now.

This book starts from a different assumption.

What if the discomfort is real?

What if it isn't personal failure, pessimism, or nostalgia — but a structural shift?

What if Britain hasn't collapsed, but has quietly moved into a different phase of life without properly acknowledging it?

This is not a book about imminent disaster. There are no predictions of chaos, revolution, or national ruin. Britain is a stable country, and it will likely remain one. The problem is not collapse. The problem is drift.

Over a long period of time, Britain has become less able to convert work into reward, taxes into services, and collective effort into visible improvement. The change has been gradual enough to avoid panic, but persistent enough to reshape everyday life. The result is a growing gap between how the country describes itself and how it feels to live in.

The central argument of this book is simple, though uncomfortable: Britain still looks like a rich country, but it no longer functions like one for a large and growing share of its population. The wealth exists, but it increasingly sits in the past — in property, accumulated assets, and inherited advantage — rather than in rising incomes, affordable living, or reliable public systems.

In other words, Britain has confused what it owns with what it earns.

For decades, this confusion didn't matter very much. Asset values rose. Globalisation was kind. Energy was cheap. Housing costs, while rising, were manageable for enough people to keep discontent muted. Weaknesses could be ignored, deferred, or explained away. There was no single moment of failure, no humiliation that forced a reckoning. Life remained broadly comfortable, and that comfort allowed problems to deepen quietly.

Avoiding crisis felt like success.

Other countries were shocked into reform — by defeat, bankruptcy, or obvious failure. Britain was not. It muddled through. It adapted just enough. It retained its institutions, its prestige, and its international voice. That continuity became a source of pride, and eventually a liability. Survival was mistaken for strength. Stability for health.

The country learned how to manage decline without ever naming it.

Now the trade-offs are harder to ignore. Housing dominates everything. Wages lag behind costs. Energy shocks bite harder than expected. Taxes rise without obvious improvement. Public services ration quietly rather than fail loudly. Politics becomes noisier while outcomes remain stubbornly unchanged. None of this feels catastrophic in isolation. Together, they create a constant sense of friction — a feeling that the system demands more while giving less back.

This book is about that friction.

It is about how a modern, developed country can remain orderly, safe, and internationally respectable while becoming progressively less workable for ordinary life. It is about how delusion can coexist with decline — not the delusion that everything is perfect, but the more subtle belief that nothing fundamental needs to change.

Britain still behaves as if it is a major player by default. It still speaks the language of leadership, influence, and exceptionalism. It still assumes its voice carries weight because it always has. In many formal senses, this remains true. Britain has nuclear weapons, a permanent seat on the UN Security Council, world-class universities, and one of the largest financial sectors on the planet.

But prestige is not prosperity. Influence is not income. And reputation does not pay the bills.

A country can remain important in the world while becoming less generous to those who live in it. It can project competence abroad while struggling to deliver it at home. It can cling to the symbols of power long after the underlying conditions that sustained them have weakened. This is the uncomfortable space Britain now occupies.

The danger is not that Britain is uniquely incompetent or corrupt. The danger is that it believes its own story. That it mistakes continuity for capability, and status for security. That it treats warning signs as noise because they do not arrive with drama.

This book does not argue that Britain is finished, broken, or beyond repair. Nor does it argue that a return to some imagined golden age is possible or even desirable. The post-war decades, the 1980s, the 1990s — each had their own distortions and exclusions. Nostalgia is not a plan.

What this book does argue is that Britain is living through the end of a particular condition: the ability to feel rich without being especially productive, to feel secure without being especially resilient, and to feel important without having to confront hard trade-offs. That condition lasted longer here than in many comparable countries, precisely because Britain was able to draw on accumulated wealth and institutional inertia.

That cushion is thinning.

The chapters that follow do not proceed as a political argument, and they are not written to flatter any ideology. Left-right debates tend to obscure more than they reveal when the issue is structural drift. Instead, this book works outward from lived experience.

It starts with the everyday questions people ask themselves: why money doesn't go as far, why work feels less rewarding, why services feel worse despite higher taxes. It then moves into the system that produced those outcomes — the asset-heavy economy, the housing trap, the productivity problem, the concentration of wealth and power. From there, it explores where this trajectory leads if left unaddressed: a more divided country, quieter rationing, lower expectations, and a growing gap between how Britain sees itself and how it is experienced.

Finally, it turns to what would actually have to change for this drift to slow or reverse — not as a manifesto, but as a set of conditions. Not promises, but trade-offs. Improvement is possible, but it would require honesty about costs, losses, and limits that British politics has long avoided.

If this book does its job properly, it should leave you with a sense of clarity rather than anger. Relief rather than despair. Relief that the unease has a shape. That the pressure has a cause. That the sense of things slipping is not imagined, and not entirely your fault.

The country has changed.

Understanding how — and why — is the first step to navigating what comes next.

Chapter 1 Why Money Doesn't Go as Far

Real UK wages in 2024 were only around 2–3% higher than in 2008.

Most people do not begin by thinking something is wrong with the country. They begin by thinking something is wrong with themselves. The money arrives, the bills are paid, the week unfolds, and somehow there is less left than there used to be. Not nothing — just less. Less margin. Less ease. Less sense that things are under control. The puzzle is subtle because life still functions. You are not destitute. You are not starving. You are not failing in any obvious way. And yet the arithmetic feels tighter than it should. This sensation is widespread precisely because it does not announce itself dramatically. It shows up as constant vigilance. As mental budgeting. As a low-level tension that never quite lifts. People assume they must have mismanaged something. That assumption is the first mistake. When millions of people experience the same quiet pressure at the same time, the problem is not individual behaviour. It is systemic.

On paper, incomes have risen. Payslips show incremental increases. Official figures suggest wages are higher than they were a decade ago. This creates the impression that people should feel better off, or at least no worse off. When that feeling does not materialise, confusion sets in. The problem lies in mistaking nominal income for real capacity. A rise in pay that is immediately absorbed by higher costs does not improve life; it merely maintains survival. Worse, it creates an illusion of progress that collapses under experience. People are told they are earning more while feeling poorer in practice. This disconnect erodes trust in explanations, statistics, and reassurance. It also encourages self-blame. If income has risen, and life feels tighter, then the fault must lie with spending habits, lifestyle choices, or personal discipline. That conclusion is understandable — and wrong. Income is only meaningful in relation to what it can buy.

Inflation is often discussed as a single number, but people do not live inside averages. They live inside necessities. The prices that rise fastest are rarely discretionary. Housing, energy, transport, food, insurance — these are not optional upgrades that can be postponed. They are the foundations of daily life. When inflation concentrates in these areas, it feels far more punishing than headline figures suggest. A modest rise in rent or mortgage payments reshapes an entire household budget. An increase in energy costs ripples outward, touching everything from groceries to commuting. These pressures accumulate quietly, month after month. Because they are unavoidable, they compress choice. People cut back elsewhere not because they want to, but because there is nowhere else to cut. Inflation here does not feel like economic theory. It feels like suffocation by small increments.

Housing is the single largest reason money no longer stretches as it once did. Rent and mortgage payments now consume a far greater share of income than they did for previous generations. This is not the result of lifestyle inflation or changing preferences. It is structural. When housing absorbs more of your earnings, everything else becomes negotiable — food quality, leisure, savings, security. The housing cost is fixed; the rest is elastic. This turns life into a series of trade-offs that used to be unnecessary. People delay milestones, avoid risk, and accept smaller ambitions because shelter has become the dominant financial priority. Housing is no longer just a place to live. It is the central organising principle of household finances. Once that shift occurs, money does not merely feel tight — it becomes strategically constrained.

Energy operates like a tax that no one votes on and no one escapes. It is embedded in heating, lighting, transport, manufacturing, food production, and logistics. When energy prices rise, they do not announce themselves once. They echo through everything else. A higher electricity bill is only the beginning. Goods cost more to produce. Services cost more to deliver. Food costs more to grow and transport. The effect is cumulative and persistent. Because energy is invisible in final prices, people struggle to trace the cause of rising costs. It simply feels as though everything is more expensive for no clear reason. This breeds frustration and resignation. Energy inflation is particularly corrosive because it undermines the sense that careful budgeting will solve the problem. You can switch suppliers, insulate, or cut usage — but the pressure remains.

Even when prices appear stable, value often is not. Products quietly shrink. Ingredients change. Durability declines. Services include fewer features or impose new conditions. This erosion rarely makes headlines because it is subtle and deniable. But over time, it changes the relationship between money and satisfaction. You pay the same amount and receive something slightly worse. That "slightly" compounds across hundreds of purchases. Consumers adapt by lowering expectations rather than protesting. This adaptation hides the scale of the loss. Official statistics struggle to capture it because quality is harder to measure than price. Yet lived experience registers it clearly. Things break sooner. Experiences feel thinner.

Convenience costs extra. Money still works — just not as well. And because the decline is incremental, it is normalised before it is noticed.

Services now demand more money while offering less certainty. Public transport is less reliable. Childcare is more expensive. Repairs take longer. Utilities require constant monitoring and negotiation. Administrative friction increases everywhere. None of this arrives as a single failure. It accumulates as background effort. People spend more time chasing, checking, comparing, and resolving issues that once ran smoothly. Time becomes the hidden cost that replaces money. When services degrade, households compensate with labour: phone calls, emails, research, contingency planning. This unpaid effort is rarely acknowledged, but it is real. Life feels busier not because people are doing more meaningful things, but because systems require more input to function at the same level. This is another way money stops going as far — it demands more of everything else to compensate.

As money stretches less, time stretches more. People travel further to find affordable housing. They commute longer to access work. They shop around endlessly to manage costs. Tasks that once took minutes now take hours. This trade-off is not freely chosen; it is imposed. Time becomes the substitute currency for affordability. But time is finite, and its loss has consequences. Fatigue increases. Stress accumulates. Capacity for long-term planning shrinks. When every decision requires optimisation, life feels brittle. This trade-off also hides inequality. Those with money can buy time; those without must spend it. Over time, this shapes not just finances, but wellbeing. A system that forces people to exchange time for survival creates exhaustion rather than resilience.

Economic indicators often suggest stability or modest improvement. Growth ticks along. Employment remains high. Inflation eventually eases. These signals are real, but incomplete. They measure aggregates, not pressure points. They average experiences that are unevenly distributed. When costs rise fastest where people cannot adjust, averages obscure pain. This disconnect leads people to distrust official explanations, not because they reject facts, but because those facts do not describe their lives. The problem is not that statistics are false. It is that they are blunt. Lived experience is granular. It registers constraint long before crisis. When policy relies too heavily on averages, it misses the slow grind that reshapes daily life. People feel dismissed rather than reassured.

Not everyone experiences this pressure equally. Younger and middle cohorts feel it most intensely. They face higher housing costs, weaker job security, and fewer buffers. Older asset-holders are partially insulated by property and savings. This divergence matters because it shapes perception. Those who are protected see stability; those exposed feel precarity. The system appears to work for some and not for others. This creates tension without a clear villain. Generational narratives emerge to explain what is, at root, an economic structure that redistributes pressure silently. Younger people are told to be patient, adaptable, resilient. Older people are told their success is earned. Both stories miss the point. The issue is not character. It is timing within a system that has changed.

People cope. They cut back. They budget. They delay. They share tips. They normalise constraint. This coping is often mistaken for resilience. In reality, it is endurance. Endurance masks deterioration by preventing visible collapse. As long as people manage, the system appears functional. But endurance has limits. It draws down reserves — financial, emotional, physical. When those reserves are depleted, problems surface suddenly and dramatically. Until then, strain remains invisible. Policymakers misread this quiet adaptation as evidence that things are "basically fine." They are not. They are being held together by individual effort substituting for systemic capacity. That substitution cannot continue indefinitely.

The question, then, is not why individuals struggle, but why the same struggle appears everywhere at once. Money does not go as far because the structure around it has changed. Costs have shifted toward essentials. Assets have absorbed income. Systems demand more effort to deliver the same outcomes. None of this is accidental, and none of it is the result of mass personal failure. Recognising this reframes the problem. It moves the conversation away from blame and toward diagnosis. The purpose of the chapters that follow is not to complain, but to explain. To show how a rich country can feel tight, how stability can coexist with strain, and why this experience is shared. If money no longer stretches, it is because the ground beneath it has moved.

Chapter 2 Higher Taxes, Worse Services

The UK tax burden rose from about 33% of GDP in 2010 to over 36% by the mid-2020s.

Life now feels busy in a way that does not translate into progress. Days are full, weeks are dense, calendars are crowded, and yet there is a nagging sense of stasis beneath the motion. People work hard, plan carefully, and adjust constantly, but the destination never seems to arrive. There is movement without momentum. Effort without lift. This creates a particular kind of unease, because it is difficult to articulate. Nothing is obviously wrong. Life is not falling apart. But neither is it opening up. The sensation is not of collapse, but of suspension. People sense they are running to stay in the same place. This feeling is widely shared, which makes it harder to dismiss as personal dissatisfaction. When millions of people feel busy but not better off, the problem lies not in motivation or ambition, but in the structure that turns effort into outcome.

Standing still often feels worse than falling. Decline is visible. It demands response. It invites change. Stagnation does neither. It requires constant vigilance just to maintain position. Economically, standing still means costs rise while rewards do not. Psychologically, it erodes morale. People can cope with hardship when they believe it is temporary or purposeful. They struggle when effort yields no clear improvement. Stagnation forces people into endless recalibration. Plans are revised downward. Expectations are quietly adjusted. Aspirations are postponed rather than abandoned, which keeps hope alive but deferred. This limbo is exhausting. It drains energy without providing closure. Over time, the absence of progress becomes its own pressure, not dramatic enough to trigger action, but persistent enough to shape behaviour and mood.

When systems stop improving, individuals are required to compensate. Growth once absorbed inefficiency and error. It created space. Without it, people become the shock absorbers. They optimise their spending, their time, their choices. They take on tasks that systems no longer perform smoothly. They bridge gaps with personal effort. This substitution is rarely acknowledged. It is framed as responsibility, resilience, or adaptability. In reality, it is unpaid labour filling a structural void. People become project managers of their own survival. This constant adjustment is not neutral. It consumes attention and capacity that could otherwise be used for creativity, risk, or rest. Over time, the accumulation of this effort becomes normalised. The system appears to function because individuals are quietly doing more to make it so.

Advancement used to be an expectation. Each generation assumed that work and patience would translate into improved living standards. That assumption has weakened. Today, the implicit goal is often simply to avoid slipping backwards. Maintaining position has replaced moving forward. This shift rarely appears in policy language or public debate. It emerges in private calculations. People aim to hold on rather than get ahead. They delay decisions that once felt safe. They treat stability as success. This redefinition happens quietly, without announcement. It becomes the background logic of adult life. When keeping up replaces getting on, ambition narrows. Risk feels irresponsible. Long-term planning becomes cautious. A society organised around maintenance rather than progress becomes conservative in the deepest sense — not politically, but psychologically.

Constant adjustment carries a cost that is rarely counted. Budgets are revisited monthly. Plans are revised annually. Expectations are recalibrated continuously. Each adjustment is small, but the cumulative effect is heavy. Mental energy is consumed by vigilance. Life becomes a series of micro-decisions about affordability, timing, and trade-offs. This constant negotiation erodes ease. Nothing feels settled. Even moments of stability feel provisional. People become adept at managing uncertainty, but that skill is not free. It replaces confidence with caution. Over time, the hidden tax of adjustment reshapes behaviour. People avoid complexity. They simplify their lives not out of preference, but necessity. The world shrinks slightly to remain manageable.

Small gains now struggle to register as victories. A pay rise is absorbed by rent. A saved expense reappears elsewhere. A resolved problem is replaced by a new one. This creates a sense that progress is illusory. Effort produces motion, but not arrival. People stop celebrating marginal improvements because experience teaches them that these will be temporary. This dampens motivation. It also distorts perception. When gains are fragile and losses persistent, optimism feels naïve. People learn not to expect improvement. They adjust emotionally as well as financially. This is not pessimism. It is adaptation to an environment where positive change rarely sticks. Over time, this adaptation becomes part of the national mood.

Stability has been quietly redefined. It no longer means comfort, security, or confidence. It means continuity. Bills paid. Crises avoided. Nothing breaking irreparably. This is a lower bar than previous generations expected, but it is increasingly treated as success. When stability is framed this way, ambition contracts. People measure life by avoidance rather than achievement. This redefinition also affects policy. Preventing deterioration becomes the goal. Improvement is treated as optional or aspirational. A society that settles for continuity risks mistaking endurance for health. It continues, but does not flourish. The difference is subtle at first. Over time, it becomes decisive.

Coping well is widely praised. People who manage under pressure are admired for resilience and competence. This praise is not misplaced, but it can be misleading. Coping well often means absorbing strain without complaint. It means adapting quietly rather than demanding change. This masks systemic problems by preventing visible failure. As long as people cope, the system appears adequate. But coping draws on finite reserves. Emotional energy, health, and confidence are slowly depleted. When those reserves run out, problems surface suddenly and dramatically. Until then, endurance is mistaken for strength. This misreading delays response and deepens eventual cost.

In the absence of structural solutions, advice culture flourishes. Financial tips, productivity hacks, lifestyle optimisation, and resilience strategies multiply. These offer practical help, but they also individualise responsibility. The message is subtle but persistent: if you struggle, you have not optimised enough. This framing fills the gap left by weak collective solutions. It reassures by offering control, but it also reinforces isolation. People focus on self-management rather than shared conditions. Advice culture thrives in environments where systems underdeliver. It provides tools for survival, not routes to change. Over time, it normalises the idea that coping is the primary task of adulthood.

Endurance becomes moralised. Those who manage are praised. Those who struggle are judged. Structural strain is reframed as personal weakness. This moral framing discourages collective action. People internalise pressure rather than externalising causes. They work harder rather than asking why effort yields so little. This suits systems that rely on quiet compliance. It also deepens inequality, as those with fewer resources are more exposed to judgment as well as strain. When endurance is treated as virtue, suffering becomes invisible. The system appears fair because failure is individualised. This is a powerful illusion.

Patience has limits. What begins as acceptance can turn into attrition. Over time, deferred plans erode confidence. People stop believing that waiting will be rewarded. Trust weakens — not explosively, but gradually. Institutions feel distant. Promises feel thin. The social contract feels vague. This erosion is difficult to measure, but easy to feel. It shows up as disengagement, cynicism, and reduced willingness to invest — emotionally, financially, or socially. A society can endure a great deal, but not indefinitely. When patience is exhausted, the response is rarely orderly.

Standing still is not neutral. It has a cost. It drains energy, narrows ambition, and reshapes expectations. It feels survivable in the short term, but corrosive over time. This chapter has described the experience. The chapters that follow will explain the mechanisms behind it. Why progress slowed. Why effort increased. Why adaptation replaced improvement. Understanding these forces does not solve them, but it reframes the problem correctly. Standing still is not stability. It is a condition that demands explanation. And once explained, it becomes harder to accept as inevitable.

Chapter 3 Working Hard, Standing Still

Average house prices have risen roughly four times faster than earnings since the late 1990s.

People sense a contradiction at the heart of modern working life. Effort has increased, expectations have risen, and demands have intensified, yet the rewards feel thinner than they once did. Work occupies more mental space, spills further into personal time, and requires constant responsiveness. Despite this, many people feel no closer to security or progress than they did years ago. This creates a quiet resentment, often directed inward. People assume they must not be pushing hard enough or making the right choices. But when increased effort fails to produce proportional reward across millions of workers, the problem cannot be individual. The paradox is not that people are lazy or disengaged. It is that the link between effort and outcome has weakened. Work feels heavier because it carries more weight without delivering more lift.

Employment figures often look healthy. Many people have jobs. Unemployment is relatively low. This creates the impression of a functioning labour market. But employment alone does not guarantee advancement. Jobs can exist without pathways. Roles can be filled without offering progression. Wages can rise nominally while stagnating in real terms. This produces a workforce that is busy but static. People are employed, but not necessarily improving their position. Careers flatten. Experience accumulates without translating into meaningful gain. The presence of work masks the absence of momentum. When employment becomes decoupled from advancement, the social promise of work changes. It stops being a route to improvement and becomes a mechanism for maintenance. This shift is subtle, but it reshapes expectations and behaviour over time.

There was a time when having a job implied more than income. It implied security, predictability, and a sense of forward motion. Work was not just something you did; it was something you built on. That implication has weakened. Today, having a job often means managing risk rather than reducing it. Security is conditional. Continuity depends on performance metrics, restructuring, or external shocks. The promise that effort would be rewarded with stability has been replaced by the expectation that stability must be continually earned. This change rarely appears in contracts, but it is widely felt. People sense that work no longer guarantees breathing room. It guarantees obligation. That difference matters. It changes how people relate to their jobs, their employers, and their futures.

Stability itself has become conditional. Contracts are more flexible. Hours are more variable. Expectations are less clearly bounded. Even in roles that appear secure, the sense of permanence is weaker. Performance is constantly assessed. Value must be demonstrated repeatedly. This creates a low-level anxiety that accompanies work everywhere. People are never quite finished. There is always another target, review, or justification. This conditionality keeps people alert, but it also keeps them tense. It blurs the line between effort and outcome. When stability is provisional, people invest more energy simply to maintain position. That energy does not translate into advancement. It is consumed by defence. Over time, work becomes less about building something and more about preventing loss.

When productivity growth is weak, pressure shifts downward. Instead of systems becoming more efficient, individuals are expected to compensate. Processes remain clumsy. Tools lag behind needs. Infrastructure strains. Rather than redesigning systems, organisations demand more from workers. People multitask, improvise, and fill gaps. This looks like flexibility, but it is often inefficiency disguised as effort. The same output requires more input. Workers feel busy because they are compensating for structural shortfalls. This creates the illusion of intensity without corresponding reward. When productivity gains are absent, there is little surplus to share. Effort increases, but returns stagnate. The burden is carried quietly by those doing the work.

A growing share of work does not count in the ways people expect. Administrative tasks expand. Reporting multiplies. Compliance grows. Coordination consumes time. None of this is inherently pointless, but much of it does not translate into higher pay or recognition. People spend more time maintaining systems rather than producing value. This labour is necessary to keep organisations functioning, but it rarely advances individual prospects. It is invisible in job titles and pay scales. Over time, people feel that their effort is being absorbed without acknowledgement. They are working harder to stand still. This disconnect fuels frustration. It also erodes pride in work, as effort becomes detached from outcome.

Professional expectations have risen steadily. Credentials matter more. Experience thresholds increase. Responsibility expands. Yet compensation often fails to keep pace. People are asked to bring more to their roles without receiving proportionally more in return. This creates a sense of imbalance. Professionalism becomes a requirement rather than a differentiator. What once commanded reward now merely grants access. This shift affects morale. People invest in education and training with the expectation of return, only to find that the return is muted. The promise of professionalisation — that skill and responsibility would be rewarded — weakens. Work feels more demanding, but not more valuable.

Advice often focuses on individual leverage. Negotiate better. Retrain. Move jobs. Relocate. For some, these strategies work. But they do not scale. When wage compression is systemic, individual manoeuvres redistribute opportunity rather than expanding it. Someone's gain becomes another's loss. The underlying structure remains unchanged. This creates a misleading narrative. Success stories are amplified. Struggle is personalised. People who cannot escape are told they failed to try hard enough. This obscures the reality that most workers operate within tight constraints. Leverage exists, but it is unevenly distributed. Treating it as universal misdiagnoses the problem.

Job-switching has become a common response to stagnation. Moving roles can deliver short-term relief. Pay bumps appear. Conditions improve temporarily. But the effect often fades. The new role exists within the same system. Costs rise. Expectations adjust. The cycle resumes. Job-hopping treats symptoms rather than causes. It also carries risk, which not everyone can afford. Over time, switching becomes less about advancement and more about damage control. It helps people keep pace, not get ahead. When movement no longer leads to progress, mobility loses its promise. Work becomes a series of lateral moves rather than an upward path.

For many, work now funds survival rather than building future security. Income is absorbed by housing, energy, and essentials. Saving becomes difficult. Planning becomes cautious. Work supports the present, but does little to secure the future. This changes the meaning of effort. When work does not accumulate into something durable, motivation shifts. People focus on coping rather than building. This is not laziness. It is rational adaptation. A system that channels effort into maintenance rather than progress reshapes ambition. People lower expectations not because they lack drive, but because the returns no longer justify risk.

Effort is widely praised. Hard work is celebrated as virtue. But outcomes receive less scrutiny. This moral framing shifts attention away from results and toward behaviour. People are told that trying hard is enough, even when it does not lead to improvement. This protects the system from critique. If effort is rewarded symbolically, failure can be individualised. Those who struggle are seen as lacking resilience rather than facing structural limits. This moralisation of effort is comforting, but misleading. It honours endurance while ignoring erosion. Over time, it trains people to accept diminishing returns as normal.

The question, then, is not why people feel tired, but why work no longer delivers what it once promised. Effort has not disappeared. Discipline has not vanished. Commitment remains. What has changed is the system that converts work into reward. Understanding this shift reframes frustration. It moves the focus away from personal inadequacy and toward structural conditions. Work has become heavier because it carries more responsibility without providing more security. The chapters that follow will examine why this happened and how it connects to wider economic change. Working harder is no longer the problem. Working harder for less is.

Chapter 4 The Housing Trap

Housing costs now take over 30% of income for many working households, compared with around 20% a generation ago.

Modern life presents itself as a landscape of choice. There are countless products, services, careers, and lifestyles on offer. Switching providers is easy. Changing jobs is encouraged. Comparison tools exist for everything. From the outside, this abundance suggests freedom and control. Yet many people experience the opposite. They make decisions constantly, but outcomes remain stubbornly similar. Costs stay high. Security remains elusive. Progress feels limited. This creates a quiet confusion. If choice is everywhere, why does life feel so constrained? The answer lies in the difference between selecting among options and shaping the conditions that define those options. Choice can exist without power. In fact, an excess of constrained choice can disguise how little room there really is to move.

Having options does not automatically confer control. Control depends on leverage. When all available options are shaped by the same underlying pressures, choosing between them changes little. You can select a different energy provider, but global prices still apply. You can move jobs, but housing costs remain fixed. You can shop around, but essentials still absorb most of your income. The presence of alternatives creates activity without agency. People feel busy making decisions, but those decisions rarely alter their position. This disconnect is exhausting. It produces the sense that life is a series of adjustments rather than a trajectory. Choice becomes a management task rather than an opportunity. The system feels dynamic, but personal circumstances feel static.

Many markets now move together. Housing, energy, transport, finance, and employment are interconnected in ways that limit real alternatives. When rents rise, wages lag. When energy costs increase, prices follow. When interest rates change, borrowing, saving, and spending all adjust at once. This synchronisation reduces the value of choice. Moving from one option to another does not escape the underlying pattern. It merely relocates you within it. People sense this intuitively. They compare notes. Different choices, similar outcomes. The market appears competitive on the surface, but structurally uniform beneath. This uniformity constrains movement. It also creates the illusion that personal decisions are decisive when they are, in reality, bounded tightly by shared conditions.

Switching has become a ritual. Change providers. Change roles. Change strategies. Movement is encouraged as a sign of agency. Sometimes it delivers relief. Often it does not. Switching creates motion without transformation. It keeps people engaged in the process of choice while leaving the structure intact. This can be psychologically reassuring. It feels active. It suggests control. But over time, repeated switching without improvement breeds cynicism. People begin to suspect that movement itself has replaced progress. They keep changing not to get ahead, but to avoid falling behind. Switching becomes maintenance rather than escape. The ritual continues because the alternative — staying still — feels worse, even when the outcome is the same.

Choice made under pressure is not free in the way it appears. Decisions are often taken quickly, under financial, emotional, or temporal constraint. People choose housing based on availability rather than preference. Jobs based on urgency rather than fit. Services based on short-term affordability rather than long-term value. These are not expressions of freedom. They are responses to pressure. When time is scarce and stakes are high, choice narrows. The appearance of options does not change the experience of compulsion. People learn to decide fast, not well. Over time, this erodes confidence. Decision-making becomes defensive. Choices are about minimising damage rather than maximising benefit. The language of choice remains, but the reality is triage.

Bad options still carry real costs. Choosing between unaffordable housing, insecure work, or unreliable services is still choosing. The consequences are not neutral. A poor choice can set someone back years. This makes decision-making stressful rather than empowering. People know that mistakes are expensive and recovery is slow. This fear further constrains choice. Risk aversion grows. People stick with suboptimal arrangements because the cost of change feels too high. The system appears flexible, but the penalties for misjudgment are severe. This creates a paradox: more choice on paper, less willingness to exercise it in practice. The space between options becomes a minefield rather than an open field.

Advice culture often assumes a level of flexibility that many people no longer possess. Guidance about careers, finance, and lifestyle presumes spare capacity — time to retrain, money to buffer transitions, energy to experiment. For some, this is realistic. For many, it is not. When advice fails, blame shifts subtly onto the individual. You had options. You chose poorly. This framing ignores the constraints that shaped the decision. It treats choice as evidence of freedom rather than as a response to pressure. Over time, people disengage from advice that does not reflect their reality. They learn that being told they have options does not mean those options are viable.

The existence of choice can become a mechanism of blame. When outcomes disappoint, the system points to the decision-maker. You chose this job. You chose this location. You chose this provider. Responsibility is individualised, even when conditions are shared. This absolves structures of scrutiny. If everyone is choosing freely, then unequal outcomes must reflect unequal decisions. This logic is powerful and misleading. It overlooks how options are shaped, limited, and priced. It also erodes solidarity. People internalise failure rather than recognising common constraints. Choice becomes a shield against critique rather than a pathway to improvement.

There is a crucial distinction between choice and power. Choice allows selection among given options. Power allows the shaping of options themselves. Most people have the former and lack the latter. They can choose how to respond, but not what they are responding to. This distinction explains much of the frustration described so far. People are active without being influential. They participate without directing outcomes. The system invites constant engagement while withholding control. This creates fatigue. It also creates a sense of futility. Participation feels compulsory, but impact feels limited. Recognising this distinction clarifies why choice alone does not deliver freedom.

Meaningful exits have narrowed. Paths that once offered escape — relocation, ownership, retraining, upward mobility — are harder to access. Each exit now carries higher costs and risks. Moving is expensive. Retraining is uncertain. Ownership requires capital. Mobility demands sacrifice. As exits close, people remain within constrained systems longer. Choice exists within the system, but leaving it becomes difficult. This traps people in cycles of adjustment. They choose, but within boundaries that rarely shift. The sense of being stuck intensifies, even as activity continues.

Constant decision-making produces fatigue. Life becomes a sequence of micro-choices, each requiring evaluation, comparison, and justification. This cognitive load drains energy. Instead of feeling empowered, people feel worn down. Decision fatigue reduces confidence and increases avoidance. People default to the familiar not because it is best, but because it is known. Over time, this reduces experimentation and reinforces existing patterns. The abundance of choice paradoxically narrows behaviour. People simplify not to gain freedom, but to survive the complexity. The system appears dynamic, but lived experience becomes repetitive.

The problem, then, is not that people lack choice. It is that they lack slack. Slack is the margin that makes choice meaningful — time, money, security, and energy. Without slack, choice is performative rather than transformative. It creates activity without agency. The chapters that follow will move from experience to explanation. They will show how slack disappeared, why systems became tight, and how choice came to substitute for power. Until slack returns, choice will continue to feel like an illusion — visible everywhere, effective nowhere.

Chapter 5 Britain's Asset Illusion

Over half of household wealth growth since 2000 has come from property price inflation, not income.

Britain still looks rich. House prices are high. Pension pots appear substantial. Financial assets dominate headlines. On paper, household wealth runs into the trillions. International comparisons still place the country among the world's richer nations. This surface prosperity matters because it shapes perception. It reassures. It suggests that whatever pressures people feel day to day must be temporary, exaggerated, or personal. How can a country that looks this wealthy be struggling? That question sits at the heart of the illusion. Visible wealth creates confidence without necessarily improving capacity. It creates the impression of success while masking fragility beneath. Britain did not become poor. It became rich in a way that does not reliably support everyday life. The contradiction between appearance and experience is not accidental. It is the defining feature of the modern British economy.

To understand this, it helps to separate two kinds of wealth that are often conflated. One is stock: what already exists. Property, land, accumulated savings, pensions, and financial assets. The other is flow: what is generated each year through work, production, and innovation. Wages, output, new value. Healthy economies grow both. Britain increasingly relied on the first while neglecting the second. Asset values rose even as income growth slowed. People felt wealthier because what they owned was worth more, not because what they earned improved their lives. This distinction matters because stock does not circulate like flow. It concentrates. It sits still. It benefits those who already hold it. Flow, by contrast, supports living standards broadly. Confusing the two allows stagnation to look like success.

For decades, rising asset values masked weak underlying growth. Property inflation substituted for productivity gains. Financial appreciation stood in for wage increases. This created a sense of momentum without expanding capacity. People borrowed against rising values to maintain consumption. Governments relied on asset-driven confidence to avoid difficult reforms. The system appeared to work. Living standards rose slowly. Crises were absorbed. But the engine was misfiring. Growth came from prices rising, not from producing more or better. This matters because asset inflation does not improve efficiency, resilience, or opportunity. It reallocates wealth without creating new value. Over time, reliance on this mechanism hollowed out the foundations of the economy while preserving the appearance of strength.

As this shift took hold, rewards flowed increasingly to ownership rather than contribution. Those who owned property or financial assets saw their wealth grow automatically. Those who relied primarily on wages did not. Returns came from scarcity rather than output. Value rose because supply was constrained, not because something new was created. This changed incentives across the economy. Capital sought reliable appreciation rather than risky expansion. Entrepreneurship became harder. Scaling became rarer. Innovation slowed. Effort still mattered, but ownership mattered more. This was not the result of a single decision or conspiracy. It emerged gradually, through choices that made sense individually. Together, they tilted the economy away from building and toward holding.

Asset wealth feels like success for powerful psychological reasons. It is visible. It can be measured. It creates a sense of security. Rising house prices feel like progress even when they increase living costs. Growing pension values feel reassuring even when future income remains uncertain. Asset appreciation flatters national narratives. It allows politicians to point to wealth while avoiding uncomfortable questions about distribution and capacity. It also feels earned, even when it is largely passive. This emotional resonance made asset-led prosperity politically attractive. Challenging it felt risky. Falling prices sound like losses, even when lower prices would improve affordability and productivity. Protecting existing value became the default position. The illusion deepened because it felt good.

As assets absorbed attention and capital, less flowed into building. Infrastructure investment lagged. Industrial capacity shrank. Housing supply failed to keep pace with demand. Money chased existing property rather than new development. This diversion had long-term consequences. Productivity growth slowed. Regional disparities widened. The economy became narrower and more concentrated. Returns depended increasingly on asset cycles rather than innovation. This was efficient in the short term and damaging in the long term. Capital followed the path of least resistance. The country accepted this because the surface indicators remained positive. The cost was paid gradually, in weaker growth, higher costs, and reduced resilience.

The consequences of this model were unevenly distributed. Asset holders were insulated. Renters and non-owners absorbed rising costs. Younger generations faced higher barriers to entry and weaker security. Timing mattered more than effort. When you were born, where you bought, and what you inherited increasingly shaped outcomes. This deepened generational divides without dramatic confrontation. The system redistributed pressure quietly. Those protected by assets experienced stability. Those outside them felt precarity. Both experiences were real. Together, they created tension without a clear villain. This unevenness made collective response harder. People lived in different economic realities within the same country.

The tax system reinforced the illusion. Income was taxed visibly and consistently. Asset gains were taxed lightly, deferred, or avoided altogether. This signalled what the system valued. Work was something to be skimmed. Ownership was something to be protected. This was rarely articulated openly, but it was felt. Incentives aligned accordingly. People sought security through assets rather than income growth. Governments relied on asset wealth to support confidence and consumption. The tax structure made this easier. Over time, this reinforced the shift away from productive investment. The system rewarded holding over building, patience over risk, preservation over expansion.

Despite these changes, the country did not feel as though it was declining. Asset wealth cushioned the experience. Rising values softened stagnation. People adapted. Life remained orderly. Institutions continued to function. The lights stayed on. Decline, such as it was, felt comfortable rather than catastrophic. This made it difficult to name. There was no collapse to respond to, only a gradual narrowing of possibility. Asset cushions allowed Britain to manage drift without confronting it. This is why the sense of strain arrived before the language to describe it. Experience shifted before narratives caught up.

Over time, this comfortable drift became a national strategy by default. Difficult reforms were postponed. Structural weaknesses were managed rather than addressed. Asset inflation did the political work of growth without requiring transformation. This worked until conditions changed. When interest rates rose, energy prices spiked, or global conditions shifted, the limits of the model became visible. Asset values could stall. Costs remained. The cushion thinned. What had felt like stability began to feel fragile. The illusion did not vanish overnight, but it cracked. The mismatch between wealth on paper and strain in practice became harder to ignore.

These cracks matter because asset-led prosperity has limits. Prices cannot rise forever. Debt cannot expand indefinitely. Demographics change. External shocks arrive. When the engine is not generating new value, resilience is weak. Britain's exposure to interest rates and global markets increased precisely because it relied so heavily on asset appreciation. When that mechanism falters, there is little else to fall back on. This is when the illusion becomes dangerous. It delays preparation and amplifies shock. What was once cushioning becomes constraining.

Prosperity, properly understood, is not about what a country owns. It is about what it can reliably produce, earn, and improve. It is about systems that convert effort into living standards and innovation into opportunity. Britain's asset illusion confused accumulation with progress. It allowed the country to look successful while becoming less adaptable. Recognising this does not require hostility to ownership or saving. It requires clarity about limits. A rich country cannot live indefinitely off past gains. It must generate new value continuously. The chapters that follow will show how Britain drifted away from that task, and what it would take to return to it.

Chapter 6 From Empire to Inertia

Britain's share of global GDP fell from around 4% in 1950 to under 3% today.

Britain did not fall in a single moment. There was no decisive defeat, no clear economic collapse, no year that marked an obvious end. Instead, the country moved from global power to something smaller through a long, gradual process that never quite announced itself. Power ebbed rather than snapped. Influence faded without disappearing. Institutions continued to function. Daily life improved enough to suggest continuity rather than rupture. This matters because societies change most decisively when they are forced to. Britain was not forced. It drifted. Decline without collapse is harder to recognise, harder to explain, and harder to confront. When nothing breaks dramatically, the instinct is to adjust rather than rethink. The result is a long period of managed diminishment that feels survivable at each step, even as the overall trajectory turns downward.

Many countries that lose great-power status experience a forcing moment. Military defeat, revolution, bankruptcy, or humiliation discredits existing systems and compels redesign. Britain avoided this. The end of empire unfolded over decades. Colonies were lost gradually. Status diminished slowly. There was no single reckoning that demanded a new national model. After the Second World War, Britain emerged battered but intact. It retained its institutions, its language, its financial centre, and much of its prestige. Living standards rose. The welfare state expanded. The country looked functional. This functional survival delayed the hardest question: what does a post-imperial economy look like when stripped of accumulated advantage and assumed importance? Without that question being forced, answers were postponed indefinitely.

Post-war recovery reinforced the illusion that the existing system merely needed adjustment. Britain rebuilt, rationing ended, and prosperity spread enough to feel meaningful. This improvement was real, but it was also misread. Survival was interpreted as success. Stability was taken as confirmation. Because things got better, deeper weaknesses were tolerated. Productivity gaps widened quietly. Industrial capacity eroded slowly. Infrastructure aged. These were manageable problems in a growing world. They did not demand transformation. Instead, they encouraged incremental repair. The country learned to fix symptoms rather than causes. Each decade passed without disaster, reinforcing the belief that fundamental change was unnecessary. This habit of interpretation shaped everything that followed.

Continuity became a national virtue. Britain's institutions evolved gradually rather than violently. Law, governance, and administration prized precedent and stability. This delivered trust and legitimacy. It also entrenched assumptions built for an earlier era. Systems designed for imperial scale and post-war growth were adjusted rather than replaced. Responsibilities accumulated. Complexity increased. Reform took the form of layering rather than redesign. This approach worked when conditions were favourable. As growth slowed and demands rose, it became a liability. Institutional continuity preserved form while capacity eroded. The state still existed, but it became less able to adapt. What once looked like steadiness began to look like inertia.

Rather than redesigning systems for a new reality, Britain adapted incrementally. Industries were privatised rather than reimagined. Finance expanded as manufacturing contracted. Consumption replaced production as a driver of growth. Each shift solved an immediate problem. None addressed the underlying question of what the economy should become. This incrementalism avoided confrontation. It also avoided coherence. Over time, the economy became narrower and more dependent on a small number of sectors. Resilience declined. Adaptation replaced strategy. Britain did not choose a new model. It assembled one accidentally, piece by piece, in response to pressure. The absence of deliberate redesign left the country with systems that worked passably in isolation but poorly together.

Britain retained symbols of power long after capacity weakened. A permanent seat on the UN Security Council. Nuclear weapons. World-class universities. A global financial centre. These symbols mattered psychologically and politically. They reinforced the sense that Britain remained a major player, even as its economic base narrowed. Prestige lingered without corresponding capacity. This mismatch shaped expectations. The country behaved as though it could still do what it once did, albeit more efficiently. Limits were acknowledged rhetorically but resisted practically. When influence is assumed rather than earned, foundations are neglected. The symbols reassured, but they also misled. They allowed Britain to overestimate what it could sustain.

The phrase "punching above our weight" captures this mindset perfectly. It acknowledges relative decline while framing it as a challenge to overcome through ingenuity rather than adjustment. Punching above your weight is admirable in sport. As a national strategy, it is risky. It encourages overreach and discourages realism. It treats limits as temporary obstacles rather than structural constraints. Britain adopted this posture across diplomacy, defence, and economics. It aimed to remain influential without fully investing in the capacity required. This worked as long as credibility held. Over time, the gap between ambition and ability widened. The strategy relied on reputation rather than renewal.

Muddling through became a model. Short-term fixes replaced long-term planning. Problems were managed rather than solved. Each crisis was treated as exceptional rather than symptomatic. This pragmatism was often praised as flexibility. In reality, it became avoidance. Muddling through works best when problems are temporary. It fails when problems are structural. Britain muddled through deindustrialisation, productivity stagnation, and regional imbalance. Each time, adaptation reduced pain enough to delay response. The absence of catastrophe removed urgency. Over decades, this produced a country skilled at coping and poor at rebuilding. The ability to muddle through became a substitute for the willingness to change.

Gradually, adaptation hardened into inertia. Systems designed to be flexible became resistant to reform. Complexity bred caution. Risk aversion increased. Change became slower and more contested. Even when problems were widely acknowledged, solutions stalled. Institutions learned to defend themselves rather than reinvent themselves. This was not malicious. It was organisational self-preservation. But the effect was the same. As conditions worsened, responsiveness declined. The country continued to function, but its ability to improve weakened. Inertia did not arrive suddenly. It accumulated quietly, one deferred decision at a time.

Reform proved difficult to sustain for predictable reasons. Costs were immediate. Benefits were delayed. Losers were visible. Winners were abstract. Political cycles were short. Institutions were fragmented. Responsibility was diffuse. Each attempt at reform encountered resistance from those who benefited from the status quo or feared disruption. Over time, reform became performative. Initiatives were announced, branded, and diluted. Structural change gave way to symbolic action. This pattern repeated across sectors. Everyone agreed something needed to change. Few were willing or able to see change through. The system learned to absorb reform without transforming.

Asset wealth and social order softened the experience of decline. Rising property values cushioned stagnation. Financialisation supported consumption. Public services strained but survived. Life remained orderly. This mattered because it removed pressure. Decline felt manageable rather than urgent. People adapted individually rather than demanding collective solutions. The country appeared stable even as capacity eroded. This stability was deceptive. It was sustained by drawing down future resilience. Asset cushions delayed reckoning, but they did not remove the need for one. The cost of delay accumulated quietly, beneath the surface of normal life.

The central problem was not decline itself. All countries change. Power shifts. Circumstances evolve. The problem was the failure to realign systems with reality. Britain carried the weight of its past into a future that no longer supported it. Expectations remained high. Capacity narrowed. Institutions lagged behind need. The reckoning was postponed because postponement was possible. Understanding this history is essential. It explains why so many current problems feel entrenched and why solutions often seem smaller than the challenges they face. Britain did not fall too fast. It fell slowly enough to avoid the moment that might have forced renewal.

Chapter 7 London and the Rest

Productivity per hour in London is roughly 30% higher than in much of the UK.

Britain increasingly feels like a country pulling in different directions. Not politically at first, but economically and experientially. People live under the same laws, pay the same taxes, and consume the same media, yet their daily realities diverge sharply depending on where they are. This is not a new observation, but it has intensified. Opportunity, income growth, and security have clustered geographically. The result is a sense that Britain no longer operates as a single, coherent economy. Instead, it functions as overlapping systems with unequal momentum. This fragmentation matters because national policy still assumes unity. Decisions are made as if conditions are broadly shared. For many people, they are not. The gap between assumed and lived reality shapes frustration, mistrust, and disengagement.

London sits at the centre of this divide. It is not just the capital, but a global city embedded in international flows of money, talent, and influence. Its economy is closely linked to other world cities rather than to much of its own hinterland. Finance, law, technology, media, and culture concentrate there. Wages at the top end are internationally competitive. Capital arrives easily. London's fortunes rise and fall with global conditions more than national ones. This gives it resilience. When Britain struggles, London often continues to attract investment and opportunity. This is not a moral failing. It is a structural position. But it means London increasingly operates on a different plane from the rest of the country, responding to different signals and pressures.

In theory, prosperous cities pull surrounding regions upward. Growth diffuses through supply chains, labour mobility, and shared infrastructure. In practice, this diffusion has been weak. London's growth has not translated into broad regional prosperity. Instead, it has often deepened disparities. High-value jobs remain concentrated. Supporting activity does not scale sufficiently elsewhere. Regions outside the capital experience slower wage growth, fewer opportunities, and weaker investment. The benefits of London's success do not spread evenly. They pool. This creates an imbalance that compounds over time. Regions fall behind not because they lack effort, but because growth is not designed to travel far. The engine runs hot, but the transmission slips.

Opportunity pulls talent inward. Ambitious young people move to London because that is where the ladders are longest. This migration is rational. It is also draining. Regions lose skilled workers, entrepreneurs, and energy. Local economies weaken further. The capital grows denser, more competitive, and more expensive. Those who remain outside face thinner labour markets and shorter career paths. This is not a failure of regional ambition. It is the result of opportunity being geographically concentrated. Over time, this hollowing out reinforces itself. Fewer opportunities mean fewer reasons to stay. Fewer people staying mean fewer opportunities emerge. The cycle tightens quietly.

Housing amplifies the divide. London's property market absorbs vast amounts of capital, domestic and international. Prices rise. Wealth concentrates. Those who own benefit. Those who do not face steep barriers. This market does not remain local. Its effects ripple outward. Rising prices in the capital pull up prices elsewhere. Policy is shaped to avoid destabilising London's housing market, even when that market drives national affordability issues. Housing becomes a national constraint anchored to one city's dynamics. Meanwhile, wages outside London rarely compensate for rising costs. The result is pressure without corresponding benefit. Housing ceases to be a local issue. It becomes a national distortion.

Public investment tends to follow success. Projects in and around London are easier to justify. Returns appear clearer. Usage is guaranteed. Political visibility is high. Investment elsewhere must fight harder for attention and funding. This is not always deliberate. It is structural. Decision-makers, institutions, and networks cluster where power already exists. Over time, this skews infrastructure, transport, and service quality. The capital accumulates advantages while other regions lag. This reinforces the perception that London matters more. People outside the capital notice. They feel overlooked not because nothing is spent, but because spending feels insufficient to change trajectory. The imbalance becomes self-reinforcing.

The gap is felt in everyday life. Access to services, transport reliability, cultural options, and professional networks often feels better in and around the capital. Elsewhere, systems feel thinner. Redundancy is limited. When something fails, there are fewer alternatives. This difference is experiential rather than ideological. It shapes how people plan, work, and cope. Those in London feel pressure and intensity. Those outside feel constraint and fragility. Neither experience is wrong. Together, they create a fractured sense of national life. People compare experiences and conclude that they are living in different countries under the same flag.

Politics reflects this proximity. Media, institutions, and careers concentrate in London. Issues that dominate life elsewhere struggle to gain sustained attention. Policy debates skew toward metropolitan concerns. This is not conspiracy. It is geography. When decision-makers live and work within one environment, it shapes perception. Over time, this creates disconnect. People outside the capital feel unseen. Trust erodes. Voting patterns shift. Cultural explanations are layered onto economic divides. The country begins to talk past itself. What feels urgent in one place feels abstract in another.

Resentment grows, but without a clear villain. London is not an enemy. Its success is real. Many outside the capital benefit indirectly from its role. This ambiguity makes frustration harder to resolve. People sense imbalance without knowing where to direct anger. This produces diffuse dissatisfaction rather than focused demand. Division deepens quietly. It is expressed culturally or politically, but rooted economically. Without a clear target, solutions remain vague. The system absorbs discontent without changing. This is a stable but unhealthy equilibrium.

London's dominance also creates vulnerability. Concentrating economic activity in one city concentrates risk. Shocks that affect London reverberate nationally. Housing downturns, financial stress, or global disruptions hit the core of the economy. A balanced country can absorb shocks regionally. A concentrated one cannot. London's success has made Britain more dependent on a narrow base. This fragility is often overlooked because the city appears strong. Strength and resilience are not the same. A system can perform well until it doesn't. Concentration raises stakes as well as returns.

Rebalancing has been attempted repeatedly. Strategies are announced. Initiatives launched. Funding pledged. Results disappoint. This is partly because rebalancing requires patience and persistence. Benefits arrive slowly. Costs are immediate. Political cycles undermine continuity. Meanwhile, the forces pulling activity toward London remain powerful. Without sustained commitment, efforts fade. The pattern repeats. Each attempt raises expectations. Each failure deepens scepticism. People learn not to believe. Rebalancing becomes rhetoric rather than reality.

Britain is not split into two hostile camps. It is stretched unevenly. The strain shows up as frustration, mistrust, and stagnation. London and the rest are bound together, but not balanced. Until opportunity, investment, and growth are distributed more evenly, this tension will persist. The country will continue to feel disjointed rather than divided. Understanding this imbalance is essential, because it feeds directly into the next problem: productivity. When growth is narrow and uneven, national productivity suffers. That is where the argument now turns.

Chapter 8 The Productivity Problem

UK productivity grew by less than 1% in total between 2008 and the early 2020s.

Productivity is one of those words that appears everywhere and explains almost nothing. It is cited in reports, speeches, and economic commentary, yet rarely unpacked in a way that connects to daily life. The term sounds technical, even abstract, which makes it easy to ignore. But productivity sits beneath almost every pressure people feel. When productivity rises, effort tends to be rewarded. When it stalls, effort becomes heavier and less effective. Britain has spent years talking around productivity without confronting it directly. This avoidance matters because productivity is not a side issue. It is the mechanism that converts work into living standards. When that mechanism weakens, the effects show up slowly, but everywhere. People feel it before they can name it.

At its simplest, productivity measures how much value is produced for a given amount of effort. When productivity improves, the same work produces more output. This creates room for higher wages, shorter hours, better services, or lower prices. When productivity stalls, none of that room exists. People can work harder without getting further ahead. This is why productivity matters to ordinary people. It determines whether effort translates into progress or merely maintenance. A country with rising productivity can improve living standards without constant strain. A country without it must choose who absorbs the cost. In Britain, that cost has increasingly been absorbed by workers, consumers, and public services rather than offset by growth.

Britain's productivity growth slowed markedly in the mid-2000s and never recovered. Compared with peer economies, output per hour stagnated. This was not a brief shock. It became a pattern. Year after year, productivity failed to accelerate. The gap with other advanced economies widened. This matters because productivity growth compounds over time. Small differences accumulate into large divergences. What began as a lag became a structural disadvantage. Britain was not suddenly inefficient. It simply stopped improving at the pace required to sustain rising living standards. The consequences unfolded gradually. Wages stagnated. Costs rose. Pressure built. The absence of crisis made the problem easier to ignore, but harder to solve.

When productivity growth is weak, effort substitutes for improvement. Workers compensate for outdated systems with time and attention. Processes that could be automated are managed manually. Infrastructure that should support efficiency becomes a source of friction. People work around problems rather than eliminating them. This creates busyness without gain. The same tasks take longer. Coordination replaces production. This is not a failure of work ethic. It is a failure of tools. When labour is not backed by adequate capital, productivity stalls. Britain asked people to work smarter without providing the means to do so. Over time, this gap widened. Effort increased. Returns did not.

Investment plays a central role here. Compared with competitors, British firms have invested less in equipment, technology, and training. This underinvestment is persistent. It reflects uncertainty, short-termism, and risk aversion. When returns appear uncertain, firms delay or avoid investment. This conservatism is rational individually and damaging collectively. Without sustained investment, productivity cannot improve. Workers cannot leverage better tools. Skills stagnate. Systems age. The economy becomes brittle. Britain's investment weakness did not cause immediate collapse. It produced slow erosion. Each year of underinvestment locked in lower potential for the next. This compounding effect is difficult to reverse once established.

Management and organisational structure also matter. Britain's economy is fragmented across sectors, regions, and firm sizes. Decision-making is often cautious. Layers of oversight multiply. Responsibility diffuses. No one intends inefficiency, but it emerges from complexity. Processes are added to manage risk. Reporting expands to ensure compliance. Each addition seems sensible. Together, they slow everything down. Productivity suffers not because people are incompetent, but because systems are overloaded. This drag is hard to quantify and easy to tolerate in the short term. Over time, it becomes a defining feature. Work becomes about navigation rather than creation.

The dominance of small firms contributes to this pattern. Small businesses are flexible and innovative, but they struggle to scale. They lack the capital, systems, and market power to invest heavily in productivity-enhancing tools. An economy dominated by small firms can be dynamic but inefficient. Britain has many such firms and relatively few that grow large. This limits diffusion of best practice. Productivity gains remain local rather than systemic. Scaling problems persist. Without pathways for firms to grow, the economy remains fragmented. Productivity improvements occur sporadically rather than broadly. This constrains national performance even as individual firms succeed.

Britain's financial sophistication did not resolve this problem. A strong financial sector can support productive investment. In Britain's case, finance often flowed toward assets rather than production. Property, financial instruments, and short-term returns attracted capital more reliably than long-term investment in capacity. This was efficient for investors and inadequate for the economy. Finance became good at allocating capital within existing structures rather than reshaping them. The link between finance and productivity weakened. This reinforced underinvestment. Capital was available, but not necessarily directed toward improving how work was done. The result was an economy rich in finance and poor in transformation.

Public sector strain fed back into productivity as well. Under-resourced services created friction for businesses and individuals alike. Transport delays, planning bottlenecks, healthcare backlogs, and education pressures all reduced efficiency. These are often treated as separate issues. In reality, they interact with productivity directly. When public systems are slow or unreliable, private effort is diverted into coping. Time is lost. Energy drains away. Productivity suffers. This feedback loop is rarely acknowledged, but it is powerful. An efficient economy depends on functioning public infrastructure. Britain's strain in this area compounded its productivity problem.

Productivity statistics can feel disconnected from experience. They lag reality. They aggregate unevenly. They obscure sectoral differences. This makes them easy to dismiss. But persistent weakness across measures signals something real. The lived experience described in earlier chapters aligns with the data. Effort has increased. Reward has not. That is what low productivity looks like in practice. The numbers are not the problem. The problem is what they reveal. Britain's difficulty has been recognising productivity as a lived issue rather than a technical one. This misrecognition delayed response.

Debates about productivity often stall because fixing it is uncomfortable. It requires long-term investment, redistribution of resources, and institutional change. Benefits arrive slowly. Costs are immediate. Winners and losers are created. Politically, this is difficult. It is easier to talk around productivity than to confront what improving it would require. Britain chose the easier path repeatedly. The result was stagnation managed through adaptation rather than resolved through change. Productivity became something to discuss rather than something to fix.

Low productivity explains much of what has come before. It connects effort to reward, work to living standards, and growth to stability. When productivity stalls, pressure spreads everywhere. Wages lag. Costs bite. Services strain. People feel busy and stuck. This is not mysterious. It is mechanical. Understanding productivity reframes the problem from moral to structural. Britain's challenge is not that people are failing. It is that the system converting effort into outcome has weakened. The cost of that weakness is felt daily. The chapters ahead will explore what happens when stagnation persists and what it would take to reverse it.

Chapter 9 Debt, Delay, and Drift

UK public debt rose from about 40% of GDP in 2007 to around 100% by the mid-2020s.

For years, debt became Britain's quiet solution to problems it did not want to confront directly. When growth slowed and wages lagged, borrowing filled the gap. This happened gradually, without drama. Debt did not arrive as an emergency measure but as a routine tool. It allowed living standards to be maintained without changing how the economy functioned. The appeal was obvious. Debt buys time. It smooths disruption. It avoids immediate pain. Britain leaned into this logic. Instead of restructuring systems or redistributing pressure, the country deferred adjustment. Borrowing became a way to preserve continuity. As long as the bills were paid and confidence held, debt seemed manageable. The deeper cost was hidden. Each year of borrowing postponed decisions while narrowing future room to manoeuvre.

Households absorbed much of this adjustment first. As wages stagnated and costs rose, credit bridged the gap. Mortgages grew larger. Terms lengthened. Consumer credit expanded. People borrowed not to speculate, but to live normally. Debt became a substitute for income growth. This normalisation mattered. Borrowing was no longer associated with crisis or extravagance. It became part of ordinary financial planning. This made the system appear stable. Consumption continued. Demand held up. But the underlying problem remained. When debt replaces income, vulnerability increases. Households become more exposed to shocks. Resilience declines quietly. What looks like stability is often leverage in disguise.

Government borrowing followed a similar pattern. Public debt rose steadily as a way to manage pressure without confronting structure. Spending cuts, tax adjustments, and borrowing were combined to keep the system functioning. Difficult reforms were postponed. Political incentives aligned with delay. Borrowing spread costs into the future, where accountability was weaker. This was not reckless in the short term. Markets tolerated it. Rates were low. The state could borrow cheaply. The danger lay in what borrowing was used for. Debt funded continuity rather than transformation. It kept services running and crises contained. It did not rebuild capacity. The bill was deferred, not reduced.

Low interest rates acted as an anaesthetic. Cheap money dulled pain and rewarded delay. Borrowing felt painless. Servicing costs were manageable. Rising debt did not translate into visible strain. This environment shaped behaviour across the economy. Governments borrowed freely. Firms refinanced. Households stretched. The system adjusted to low rates as a permanent condition. This encouraged complacency. When money is cheap, urgency fades. Structural weaknesses can be tolerated longer. Britain learned to live with its problems because they did not hurt enough to force change. The anaesthetic worked until it didn't. When rates rose, sensation returned abruptly.

Crucially, much of this borrowing did not fund transformation. It supported consumption, asset prices, and existing systems. Debt can be productive if it builds capacity. In Britain's case, it often preserved the status quo. Infrastructure investment lagged. Productivity gains were modest. The economy did not become significantly more efficient. Borrowing bought time without buying improvement. This distinction matters. Debt that transforms creates future ability to repay. Debt that preserves merely postpones reckoning. Britain accumulated the latter. Each year of delay increased dependence on favourable conditions continuing indefinitely.

The costs of this strategy were shifted forward. Future taxpayers inherited obligations created to maintain present comfort. This intergenerational transfer was rarely discussed explicitly. It happened by default. Younger generations entered a world with higher debt, higher asset prices, and weaker growth. They paid more to access the same fundamentals. This transfer was not the result of malicious intent. It was the outcome of delay. When societies choose continuity over adjustment, the future absorbs the cost. This creates quiet resentment. People sense unfairness without a clear moment of betrayal. The imbalance accumulates invisibly until it shapes attitudes and trust.

Debt felt painless for psychological reasons as well as financial ones. Numbers grew abstract. Trillions became normalised. As long as daily life continued, concern remained low. Politically, debt lacks a natural constituency of opposition. Benefits are immediate and diffuse. Costs are delayed and impersonal. This asymmetry favours borrowing. It also discourages honesty. Talking about debt as a trade-off invites discomfort. Framing it as management avoids it. Britain became adept at the latter. The language of sustainability replaced the language of change. Debt became background noise rather than a signal.

Asset inflation reinforced this dynamic. Rising property values created collateral. Borrowing appeared safer. Leverage increased quietly. Debt and asset prices fed each other. Higher prices justified larger loans. Larger loans supported higher prices. This cycle sustained confidence. It also deepened fragility. When leverage rises faster than capacity, systems become sensitive to shocks. Britain's reliance on this dynamic made it vulnerable to rate changes and external disruption. The illusion of wealth masked the build-up of risk. Debt did not feel dangerous because assets appeared to cover it. This balance depended on conditions remaining favourable.

Delay became habitual. Decisions were deferred because deferral worked. Each postponed reform reduced immediate pain. This reinforced the strategy. Delay felt responsible. Acting decisively felt risky. Over time, postponement became policy culture. Problems were acknowledged but not resolved. Reviews were commissioned. Strategies were announced. Implementation lagged. This pattern extended across housing, infrastructure, productivity, and public services. Delay was not paralysis. It was active management of decline. The system functioned, but it did not improve. Drift set in because there was no forcing moment to interrupt it.

As debt accumulated, future options narrowed. Higher debt constrained fiscal space. Rising interest rates increased servicing costs. Choices became harder. Trade-offs sharpened. What once felt flexible became rigid. Delay reduced freedom. Each year of borrowing limited the next year's choices. This is the paradox of debt-led stability. It preserves options in the short term while eliminating them in the long term. Britain entered the present with fewer tools than it might have had. The room to manoeuvre shrank quietly. When pressure returned, it did so with greater force.

Eventually, the bill arrives. Rising interest rates, energy shocks, and global instability exposed the limits of delay. Costs that had been manageable became painful. Debt servicing rose. Households felt strain. Governments faced hard choices. The anaesthetic wore off. What had been postponed could no longer be ignored. This moment did not arrive as a single crisis. It arrived as a series of pressures that made drift unsustainable. The system that had relied on borrowing to smooth change now had to confront accumulated constraints.

Debt bought Britain time. It did not buy renewal. Delay preserved comfort while capacity eroded. Drift replaced direction. Understanding this sequence is essential. It explains why pressures now feel simultaneous and severe. Debt was not the cause of decline, but it shaped how decline was managed. It allowed Britain to avoid confrontation with reality for longer than most countries. That avoidance carried a price. The next chapters will explore what happens when time runs out and what choices remain when delay is no longer available.

Chapter 10 When the Social Contract Frays

Home ownership among under-35s has fallen from around 60% in the early 1990s to under 40%.

For much of the post-war period, Britain operated under an unspoken agreement. Work hard, play by the rules, contribute through taxes and effort, and life would, over time, get better. It was not a promise of riches, but of progress. Each generation expected to live a little better than the last. Security was cumulative. Patience was rewarded. This contract shaped behaviour and belief. It encouraged compliance because compliance made sense. People accepted obligation because it was paired with improvement. The agreement was never written down, but it was widely understood. It structured expectations about work, housing, family, and the future. When that understanding holds, societies are stable. When it weakens, strain appears not as rebellion at first, but as confusion. People keep doing their part and quietly wonder why the outcome has changed.

Over time, the link between effort and security loosened. Doing the right thing no longer guaranteed stability, let alone advancement. Work remained demanding. Rules remained firm. But the rewards became uncertain. People followed prescribed paths and found themselves exposed anyway. Jobs did not ensure housing security. Saving did not guarantee affordability. Loyalty did not ensure continuity. This erosion happened gradually, making it harder to identify. There was no single moment when the contract broke. Instead, it thinned. Each disappointment adjusted expectations downward. People learned to hope less, plan cautiously, and assume fragility. This adaptation was rational. It was also corrosive. When effort stops producing predictable security, faith in the system weakens, even if behaviour remains compliant.

Obligations, however, did not loosen. Taxes were still collected. Rules were still enforced. Compliance was still expected. What changed was the certainty of return. Protections became conditional. Services became strained. Support was harder to access. The asymmetry mattered. A contract where duties are firm but benefits are uncertain feels one-sided. People sense imbalance even when they cannot articulate it. This does not immediately lead to refusal. It leads to recalibration. People give what they must and withdraw what they can. Trust becomes transactional. Participation becomes minimal rather than wholehearted. The system continues to function, but enthusiasm fades. This quiet shift alters the character of society long before it alters behaviour visibly.

Belonging itself became conditional. Security depended increasingly on constant performance — staying employed, remaining productive, avoiding disruption. Safety nets existed, but they felt thinner and more bureaucratic. Falling behind carried stigma as well as risk. This conditionality reshaped identity. People learned to present themselves as competent and coping, even when they were strained. Vulnerability became dangerous. The message was subtle but persistent: belonging must be earned continuously. This undermined solidarity. When everyone feels one misstep away from trouble, empathy shrinks. People focus inward. Collective identity weakens. The social contract shifts from shared assurance to individual management of risk.

Trust erodes quietly. Institutions do not need to fail spectacularly to lose legitimacy. They only need to disappoint consistently. Delays, complexity, and inconsistency accumulate. People stop expecting help to arrive quickly or at all. They adjust behaviour accordingly. This erosion is difficult to reverse because it is not dramatic. There is no clear betrayal to address. Instead, there is a general sense that institutions are stretched, distracted, or indifferent. People lower expectations. They stop asking. This withdrawal is polite and orderly, which makes it easy to overlook. But it matters. Trust is a form of social capital. When it drains away, systems become harder to operate effectively.

Frustration does not disappear when trust weakens. It looks for outlets. Often, it surfaces culturally or politically rather than economically. People argue about identity, values, or symbols. These debates carry emotional charge because they stand in for deeper unease. Economic frustration is displaced into cultural conflict because it lacks a clear target. Structural problems are abstract. Cultural ones are tangible. This misdirection is not accidental. It is easier to fight over visible differences than to confront diffuse constraints. The result is noise without resolution. Anger circulates, but the source remains largely untouched. This creates the impression of division without addressing its cause.

Despite this, most people continue to comply. They follow rules, pay taxes, and show up. What changes is belief. Compliance becomes habitual rather than consensual. People do what is required without trusting the system to reciprocate. This hollowing out is dangerous because it is invisible.

Institutions rely not just on obedience, but on legitimacy. When belief fades, systems become brittle. They function until stressed. Under pressure, compliance without belief collapses quickly. The difference between a society that believes and one that merely complies is not apparent in calm periods. It becomes decisive in crisis.

Where possible, people opt out. They seek private solutions to public problems. They pay for services, insulate themselves, or disengage. Some withdraw socially. Others lower ambition. This opting out is uneven. Those with resources escape pressure. Those without remain exposed. This deepens inequality and resentment. It also weakens shared systems further, as support drains away. Opting out feels rational individually. Collectively, it is corrosive. Public systems depend on broad participation. When confidence drops, so does willingness to invest emotionally or financially. The social contract frays not because people reject it, but because they stop relying on it.

Solidarity becomes harder to sustain. Shared sacrifice requires shared belief. When people doubt that burdens and benefits are distributed fairly, willingness to contribute declines. Appeals to duty ring hollow. Cooperation becomes conditional. This affects everything from taxation to public service support. People ask what they get in return. This is not selfishness. It is a response to uncertainty. When outcomes feel unpredictable, people protect themselves. The collective weakens as a result. This dynamic is subtle but powerful. It does not announce itself. It accumulates until shared projects feel implausible.

Generational misunderstanding compounds the problem. Different cohorts experience different versions of the contract. Older generations may remember progress and security. Younger ones inherit precarity and delay. Each interprets the other through their own experience. Frustration turns into judgment. Empathy erodes. This misunderstanding is not about values. It is about lived reality. When people grow up under different conditions, they develop different expectations. Without recognising this, dialogue fails. The contract frays further because it is no longer even understood in the same way by everyone.

Cohesion weakens before collapse. Social bonds stretch long before institutions fail. People continue to function, but connection thins. Participation becomes procedural. Belief recedes. This is the danger zone. It feels stable enough to ignore and fragile enough to break under stress. Britain now occupies this space. The fraying social contract is not a conclusion. It is a warning. It signals that the old assumptions no longer hold. The chapters ahead will examine what happens when this warning is ignored — and what choices remain when belief cannot be taken for granted.

Chapter 11 Politics Without Fixes

Major infrastructure projects in the UK overrun initial budgets by an average of 30–50%.

Politics in Britain now feels constant. News cycles churn, debates rage, leaders come and go, and yet many of the same material problems persist year after year. Housing remains scarce. Productivity remains weak. Public services remain strained. This creates a sense of motion without repair. People are not disengaged because politics is absent; they are disengaged because it feels ineffective. The volume of politics masks the lack of resolution. Arguments repeat. Promises recycle. Outcomes disappoint. This disjunction matters because it erodes belief in politics as a mechanism for improvement. When politics feels busy but unproductive, it trains people to expect performance rather than progress. Over time, attention shifts from what is being fixed to who is winning the argument. Politics becomes a spectacle rather than a tool.

As trust weakened, politics became more performative. Messaging took precedence over delivery. Identity and positioning replaced problem-solving. This shift was not cynical at first. It was adaptive. When belief declines, persuasion becomes harder. Leaders compensate by amplifying narrative. They signal values, allegiance, and intent more loudly because results are slower and less visible. Over time, this emphasis hardens. Success is measured in headlines rather than outcomes. Policy becomes a prop. Announcements substitute for implementation. The gap between rhetoric and reality widens. People sense this instinctively. They learn to discount promises. Performance escalates to compensate, further crowding out substance. The system feeds on attention rather than resolution.

Structural problems require time. Infrastructure takes years. Productivity reform takes decades. Education and health outcomes unfold slowly. Politics, by contrast, operates on short cycles. Elections, media scrutiny, and internal party dynamics reward immediacy. This mismatch distorts incentives. Leaders prioritise actions that show quick impact, even if those impacts are superficial. Long-term projects are launched and abandoned. Continuity is rare. Each new administration seeks differentiation rather than persistence. This churn undermines progress. Problems that require patience are addressed impatiently. The result is fatigue without improvement. People experience policy as a series of resets rather than a sustained effort. This weakens confidence that politics can handle long horizons.

Policy churn becomes a substitute for change. Reviews are commissioned. Strategies are published. Initiatives are branded and rebranded. Each creates activity. Few survive long enough to mature. This creates the appearance of responsiveness without the substance of delivery. Churn absorbs energy. Institutions adapt to it. Staff learn to wait out reforms rather than embed them. The system becomes skilled at change without transformation. This is not sabotage. It is survival. When policy is unstable, implementation becomes cautious. Risk is avoided. Over time, churn itself becomes a barrier. Real change requires continuity. Constant reform prevents it. Politics mistakes motion for progress and then wonders why outcomes do not improve.

A central feature of this paralysis is the avoidance of trade-offs. Leaders promise outcomes without acknowledging costs. Growth without pain. Services without tax. Change without disruption. This is understandable in a competitive political environment. But it is corrosive. Trade-offs exist whether they are acknowledged or not. When they are denied, they reappear as failure. Projects stall. Budgets strain. Expectations collapse. Voters are left confused and disappointed. Over time, this pattern trains people not to believe. Politics becomes a theatre of impossibility. Each promise feels less credible than the last. The refusal to speak honestly about limits undermines the very authority leaders seek to preserve.

Blame fills the gap left by delivery. Responsibility is shifted sideways and backwards. Predecessors, opponents, institutions, global forces — all are invoked to explain failure. Some of this is fair. Context matters. But blame becomes currency when solutions are scarce. It rallies supporters and deflects scrutiny. It also entrenches division. When politics is framed as a contest of fault rather than a process of repair, cooperation collapses. Each side guards its narrative. Shared problems become partisan weapons. This makes sustained reform harder. Blame clarifies identity but obscures solutions. It keeps politics loud and shallow.

Competence lost appeal in this environment. Managerial competence became associated with maintaining the status quo rather than improving it. Stability came to look like stagnation. This created space for disruption and spectacle. Voters sought energy rather than expertise. This was not irrational. When systems fail to deliver, continuity feels complicit. But rejecting competence carries risk. Disruption without capacity creates volatility. Governance becomes harder. The system oscillates between management and revolt without achieving either transformation or stability. Competence alone cannot inspire, but its absence is costly. Politics struggles to reconcile these needs in an era of low trust.

Disagreement over facts further undermined governance. Shared reality fractured. Data, expertise, and evidence became contested terrain. This was not simply misinformation. It reflected deeper distrust. When institutions fail to deliver, their authority erodes. Facts associated with them lose legitimacy. Policy-making depends on shared understanding. Without it, debate becomes circular. Each side cites its own sources. Decisions lack foundation. Implementation falters. This epistemic breakdown is subtle but severe. It does not stop politics. It stops problem-solving. When reality itself is disputed, policy becomes narrative rather than response.

Technocratic solutions failed to inspire because they lacked visible impact. Expert-led reforms promised efficiency and optimisation. They often delivered incremental improvement at best. In a context of stagnation, this felt insufficient. Expertise became associated with caution and delay. People did not reject expertise per se. They rejected its apparent inability to change outcomes. This delegitimised technocracy without replacing it with something better. Politics drifted between expert management and populist critique, satisfying neither. The absence of tangible progress made every approach feel hollow. The system lost its centre of gravity.

Populism emerged as a symptom of this environment, not its cause. It channelled frustration into simple narratives and clear enemies. It promised restoration without detail. This appeal made sense in a system perceived as unresponsive. Populism offered recognition rather than resolution. It named grievances even if it could not solve them. This energy disrupted politics but did not rebuild it. Governing proved harder than campaigning. Expectations rose faster than capacity. Disappointment followed. The cycle repeated. Populism did not break the system. It exposed its weakness.

Institutions now govern without deep belief. Procedures continue. Laws are enforced. Budgets are passed. But legitimacy is thinner. Compliance persists, belief recedes. This hollowing out is dangerous because it leaves little margin for crisis. Systems rely on goodwill in emergencies. When belief is low, response falters. Britain has not reached collapse. It has reached fragility. The machinery still runs, but confidence in its direction is weak. This is the political counterpart to the economic stagnation described earlier. Function without faith cannot endure indefinitely.

This chapter marks the end of diagnosis. Politics without fixes is not a temporary phase. It is the product of delayed decisions and accumulated constraints. The system now faces a choice. Continue managing decline through performance and postponement, or confront the costs of renewal openly. Part IV turns to that choice. What would have to change? What would need to be rebuilt? And what would honesty look like in a country that has lived for decades without a forcing moment?

Chapter 12 Facing Reality

......

Britain has become skilled at partial honesty. Problems are acknowledged in broad terms, often eloquently, but their implications are softened or deferred. Productivity is discussed, but not confronted. Decline is hinted at, but rarely named. This halfway realism creates comfort without clarity. It allows agreement without consequence. Everyone can nod along without accepting what change would require. Partial honesty is appealing because it preserves dignity. It avoids panic. It reassures. But it also blocks action. When problems are described without their scale or urgency, solutions remain cosmetic. Britain has spent years diagnosing symptoms while avoiding prognosis. Facing reality means moving beyond acknowledgement to acceptance. That step is harder because it forces choices. Partial honesty delays those choices. At this stage, delay is itself a decision.

Realism often feels like pessimism in Britain because it challenges inherited expectations. To say that capacity has shrunk, that options are limited, or that trade-offs are unavoidable sounds defeatist in a country accustomed to global relevance. Optimism is culturally preferred. Resilience is celebrated. Decline is treated as a failure of attitude rather than a material condition. This framing makes realism suspect. It feels like surrender rather than preparation. Yet realism is not about lowering ambition. It is about aligning ambition with capacity. Without that alignment, ambition becomes performative. Britain's difficulty is not that it lacks hope, but that it resists recalibrating it. Preparation requires naming limits. That naming feels uncomfortable precisely because it breaks with familiar narratives.

The most persistent distortion comes from pretending Britain remains exceptional in ways that no longer apply. Exceptionalism once rested on industrial dominance, imperial reach, and financial power. Those foundations have changed. Influence remains, but it rests on thinner economic substance. Clinging to past status shapes decisions subtly. It encourages overcommitment abroad and underinvestment at home. It frames restraint as weakness. It delays adjustment. Exceptionalism becomes a story that justifies continuity rather than change. This does not mean Britain is irrelevant or powerless. It means that power must be understood differently. Letting go of comforting myths is not self-denial. It is strategic clarity. Nations that misread themselves act poorly. Britain has been misreading itself for too long.

A crucial distinction must be restored: influence is not the same as capacity. Britain retains diplomatic presence, cultural reach, and institutional voice. These matter. But they do not substitute for economic strength, productive capacity, or resilience. Influence without capacity depends on credibility. When capacity erodes, influence becomes brittle. Decisions are made based on assumed weight rather than actual support. This creates strain. It also creates exposure. Britain has often behaved as though presence alone confers power. In reality, presence must be backed by substance. Facing reality means rebalancing attention away from symbols and toward foundations. Influence can be rebuilt. Capacity must be rebuilt first.

Scale matters again. Many of Britain's challenges are too large for incremental fixes. Housing shortages, productivity gaps, regional imbalance, and infrastructure decay require sustained, coordinated effort. Small adjustments will not accumulate fast enough. Yet British policy culture favours marginal change. Big moves feel risky. They attract opposition. They demand trade-offs. But avoiding scale guarantees inadequacy. The mismatch between problem size and response size explains much of the frustration described earlier. Facing reality means accepting that meaningful improvement will be visible, contested, and disruptive. That disruption is not failure. It is evidence that change is real. Scale cannot be avoided indefinitely.

Comforting myths persist because they provide emotional stability. Stories about muddling through, quiet competence, and national resilience have served Britain well in the past. They now inhibit renewal. Letting go of them feels like losing part of national identity. This resistance is human. It is also costly. Myths that once unified can later constrain. Facing reality requires emotional as well as technical adjustment. It asks people to accept that the past is not a template for the future. That acceptance does not erase history. It frees the present. Countries that renew successfully do not cling to stories that no longer fit. They write new ones.

Honesty is a prerequisite for reform. Technical solutions cannot succeed without narrative reset. People need to understand why change is necessary and what it will cost. Without that understanding, reform lacks legitimacy. Britain has often attempted reform without honesty. Benefits were promised without sacrifices named. This pattern bred disappointment and mistrust. Facing reality means speaking plainly about trade-offs. It means acknowledging losers as well as winners. This is politically difficult, but unavoidable. Reform without honesty fails quietly. Reform with honesty may fail loudly, but it has a chance. At this stage, chance matters more than comfort.

Other countries have faced similar moments. Some confronted limits directly. They accepted smaller roles, rebuilt capacity, and refocused internally. They invested heavily, restructured institutions, and tolerated short-term pain for long-term gain. These examples are not blueprints. Context differs. But the pattern is instructive. Renewal followed realism. Where denial persisted, stagnation deepened. Britain is not uniquely trapped. It is simply late to confront its position. Learning from others does not diminish sovereignty. It enhances it. Facing reality includes recognising that adjustment is not shameful. It is common.

Doing nothing is no longer neutral. Drift now carries increasing risk. Demographics tighten. Debt constrains. Global competition intensifies. The margin for error shrinks. Strategies that once bought time now consume it. Inaction will not preserve stability. It will erode it. The costs of delay are rising faster than the costs of change. This inversion marks a turning point. Britain has crossed from manageability into fragility. Facing reality means recognising that waiting is itself a gamble — and not a favourable one. The absence of crisis should not be mistaken for safety.

The window for adjustment is narrowing. An ageing population increases pressure on services. Debt servicing absorbs resources. Geopolitical instability raises stakes. These forces reduce flexibility. Choices that could have been gradual now require urgency. This does not mean panic. It means prioritisation. Not everything can be fixed at once. Facing reality means deciding what matters most and committing to it. Delay fragments effort. Focus concentrates it. Britain has lacked focus because it has avoided hierarchy of needs. The next phase requires one.

Realism does not require despair. Naming limits is an act of agency. It allows deliberate choice rather than reactive coping. Countries that accept their constraints can still prosper. They align ambition with capacity and rebuild systematically. Britain retains assets: institutions, skills, legitimacy, and social cohesion, albeit strained. These can support renewal if mobilised honestly. Facing reality is not about accepting decline. It is about refusing illusion. Illusion narrows options. Realism expands them by grounding action in truth.

This chapter sets the terms for what follows. Renewal begins with clarity. The chapters ahead will outline what must change — not as aspiration, but as requirement. They will be concrete, demanding, and uncomfortable. That is unavoidable. Britain's future depends less on optimism than on alignment between story and structure. Facing reality is the first act of rebuilding. Without it, nothing that follows can hold.

Chapter 13 Rebuilding the Economic Base

UK investment has averaged around 17% of GDP, compared with over 20% in comparable economies.

Every serious reform rests on the same foundation: a productive economic base. Without it, redistribution becomes brittle, public services strain, and social promises collapse under their own weight. Britain has spent years attempting to adjust outcomes without rebuilding the base that generates them. This cannot work indefinitely. You cannot sustainably improve wages, services, or security without increasing what the economy produces and how reliably it does so. The base is not an abstract concept. It is the machinery that turns effort into value. When that machinery weakens, everything built on top becomes fragile. Rebuilding the economic base is therefore not one reform among many. It is the prerequisite for all others. Without it, change remains cosmetic. With it, change becomes possible.

For too long, Britain treated consumption as a substitute for production. Spending kept demand alive even as capacity eroded. Households borrowed. Governments borrowed. Imports filled gaps. This created the appearance of activity without the substance of growth. Consumption feels dynamic because money moves. But if what is consumed is not produced domestically, the benefits leak away. Britain relied on this model because it was politically easier. It postponed conflict. It supported living standards temporarily. But it did not rebuild capacity. Consumption is an outcome, not a strategy. Treating it as a driver confused effect with cause. Rebuilding the base means reversing that logic. Production must lead. Consumption must follow.

"Making things" no longer means only factories and assembly lines. Production today includes energy generation, data infrastructure, software, logistics, advanced services, and skills systems. It includes how efficiently ideas move from conception to scale. Britain often frames production narrowly and nostalgically. This limits imagination. Rebuilding capacity requires recognising modern forms of value creation and supporting them deliberately. It also requires accepting that production is systemic. It depends on networks, standards, and coordination. You cannot bolt it on after the fact. Britain must rebuild its productive systems as integrated wholes rather than isolated projects. This demands coherence, not nostalgia.

Investment must become a habit rather than an event. Britain excels at launching initiatives and announcing funds. It struggles to sustain commitment over time. Productive capacity grows through consistent investment, not bursts. Stop-start funding discourages scale. Firms hesitate. Skills pipelines falter. Infrastructure degrades. Rebuilding the base requires predictable, long-term capital allocation. This applies to both public and private investment. The goal is not spectacle but accumulation. Capital must be deployed patiently, year after year, through cycles. Without this discipline, productivity gains remain sporadic. Habitual investment builds confidence. Confidence unlocks scale.

Patient capital is essential. Britain's financial system is sophisticated, but often oriented toward quick returns. Asset speculation has crowded out long-term productive investment. Patient capital behaves differently. It tolerates slower payoff. It supports scaling. It invests in systems rather than extraction. Rebuilding the base requires shifting incentives toward this form of capital. This does not mean rejecting markets. It means aligning them with long-term capacity building. Pension funds, development banks, and public-private vehicles can play a role. But the principle matters more than the mechanism. Capital must be rewarded for building, not merely owning. Without patient capital, production remains shallow.

Reindustrialisation is necessary, but nostalgia is dangerous. Britain cannot recreate the industrial landscape of the past. Nor should it try. The goal is not to restore lost jobs, but to rebuild capability. Modern industry is capital-intensive, skill-intensive, and networked. It requires different planning, different training, and different expectations. Reindustrialisation must focus on where Britain can build advantage now, not where it once dominated. This requires humility and analysis. It also requires resisting the temptation to promise easy wins. Rebuilding capacity is slow. Pretending otherwise repeats old mistakes.

Energy sits at the base of everything. Affordable, reliable energy underpins productivity across sectors. Britain's energy system has become a source of vulnerability rather than strength. Volatility raises costs everywhere. Dependence constrains policy. Rebuilding the base requires treating energy as economic infrastructure, not merely environmental policy. Investment in generation, storage, and grids is foundational. This is not ideological. It is practical. Every productive activity depends on energy. Without secure supply, everything else is compromised. Energy policy is industrial policy, whether acknowledged or not.

Infrastructure enables scale. Transport, planning systems, digital connectivity, and logistics determine whether firms can grow beyond local markets. Britain's infrastructure gaps constrain expansion. Planning delays stall investment. Transport bottlenecks fragment labour markets. Digital systems lag. These frictions accumulate. Individually, they seem manageable. Collectively, they suppress productivity. Rebuilding the base requires removing these constraints deliberately. Infrastructure is not just about speed. It is about reliability and predictability. Firms invest where systems work. People move where access exists. Scale emerges where friction is low.

Britain celebrates start-ups but neglects scale-ups. Starting a business is only the first step. Growth requires capital, talent, markets, and support. Too many British firms stall before reaching meaningful size. This limits productivity and wages. Rebuilding the base requires focusing on firms that can grow, export, and anchor supply chains. This means different support structures, procurement policies, and financial instruments. It also means tolerating failure as part of growth. Scale cannot be achieved without risk. Britain must decide whether it wants many small firms or fewer large, productive ones. The answer matters.

Regional capacity is national strength. Concentrating production in one area increases vulnerability. Spreading it builds resilience. Britain's imbalance weakens the base. Rebuilding capacity across regions reduces pressure on the centre and expands opportunity elsewhere. This is not charity. It is strategy. Regional economies with productive capacity stabilise national output and absorb shocks. Investment must follow this logic consistently, not rhetorically. Capacity grows where commitment persists. Regional rebuilding requires trust and patience. It cannot be announced and abandoned.

Rebuilding the economic base will be disruptive. It will challenge existing interests. It will change landscapes. It will require trade-offs. This disruption should not be avoided. It should be managed. Comforting everyone preserves stagnation. Visible change signals seriousness. Britain must accept that rebuilding will be contested and uneven. The alternative is continued drift. Disruption is not failure. It is evidence that the base is being reshaped rather than merely discussed.

This chapter marks the pivot from diagnosis to construction. Rebuilding the economic base provides direction where drift dominated. It anchors reform in capacity rather than narrative. Without this anchor, other changes will not hold. With it, renewal becomes feasible. The chapters that follow will build on this foundation, addressing labour, skills, institutions, and governance. None of them work in isolation. Together, they form the structure Britain has postponed building for too long.

Chapter 14 Work, Wages, and Dignity

Median pay grew more slowly than inflation for much of the 2010s.

Any economic system that asks people to work must ensure that work reliably pays. Not extravagantly, not uniformly, but predictably enough to support a stable life. When effort does not translate into security or progress, the system fails in both moral and practical terms. Britain's problem is not that people refuse to work. It is that work no longer guarantees dignity. People show up, comply, adapt, and contribute, yet remain anxious about housing, bills, and the future. This erodes motivation and trust. A system that relies on effort while failing to reward it steadily cannot sustain legitimacy. Restoring the link between work and security is not an optional improvement. It is a requirement for economic function and social cohesion. Without it, productivity stalls and belief drains away.

Wages have drifted away from living costs. Pay may rise nominally, but essentials rise faster. Housing absorbs income. Energy drains budgets. Transport, childcare, and food tighten margins. This gap is not accidental. It reflects years of policy choices that treated wages as flexible while allowing costs to inflate. The result is quiet compression. People work more for less effective reward. Dignity suffers not because people expect luxury, but because they cannot plan. When income barely covers essentials, autonomy shrinks. Choices narrow. Life becomes reactive. This is corrosive. A society where wages do not anchor living standards produces insecurity by design. Restoring alignment between pay and cost is foundational, not redistributive indulgence.

In-work poverty is the clearest signal of systemic failure. When people who follow the rules and remain employed cannot meet basic needs, the problem lies beyond individual behaviour. Britain increasingly relies on work that does not sustain life. This is often reframed as a problem of hours, skills, or personal budgeting. These explanations avoid the core issue. Work itself has been devalued. In-work poverty shifts responsibility from system to individual, masking structural imbalance. It also damages productivity. People under constant financial stress cannot perform optimally. They manage survival rather than contribute fully. Tolerating in-work poverty undermines the very economy that depends on labour. It is not efficient. It is extractive.

Wage restraint has long been justified as necessary for competitiveness. Suppressing pay was presented as a way to attract investment and protect jobs. In practice, it weakened demand and productivity. Low wages discourage investment in skills and technology. They reward labour substitution over innovation. An economy that competes on low pay competes against itself. Britain followed this logic implicitly for years. The result was stagnant wages and weak productivity growth. Competitiveness built on wage suppression is fragile. It relies on people absorbing pressure indefinitely. That capacity has limits. Reconnecting competitiveness to quality, efficiency, and value creation requires abandoning the reflex of restraint.

Productivity and pay must reconnect. When output rises and wages do not, incentives distort. Workers disengage. Trust erodes. Productivity gains must be shared to sustain momentum. This is not ideological. It is functional. Systems where gains flow upward exclusively eventually stall. Britain's productivity problem cannot be solved without addressing distribution. Higher output that bypasses workers does not stabilise the system. It intensifies resentment. Rebuilding the base means ensuring that productivity improvements translate into visible reward. Without that link, calls for efficiency sound hollow. People will not invest effort in a system that captures its returns elsewhere.

Individual bargaining cannot substitute for collective leverage. Advice to negotiate harder ignores structural imbalance. Many workers lack credible alternatives. Markets dominated by large employers concentrate power. Collective mechanisms exist to balance this. Britain weakened them over time. The result was fragmentation. Individuals were asked to carry the burden of negotiation alone. This favours those already advantaged. Restoring bargaining power does not require recreating past models wholesale. It requires recognising that labour markets are not neutral. Power shapes outcomes. Rebalancing that power supports fair wages and stability. Without collective leverage, dignity becomes conditional on position rather than contribution.

Security is not the enemy of productivity. It is an input. People perform better when they are not constantly defending their position. Stable contracts, predictable hours, and clear expectations improve focus and investment in skills. Insecure work may offer flexibility for employers, but it imposes hidden costs on the system. Turnover rises. Training is wasted. Commitment declines. Britain often treats insecurity as efficiency. This misreads human behaviour. Productivity depends on trust and continuity. Security allows people to plan, invest, and improve. Treating it as indulgence undermines performance. Dignity at work is not a luxury. It is infrastructure.

Flexibility and dignity are often framed as opposites. This is a false trade-off. Work can be adaptable without being precarious. Flexibility that shifts all risk onto workers is not flexibility. It is exposure. Genuine adaptability requires shared risk and shared reward. Britain embraced flexibility unevenly. Employers gained optionality. Workers absorbed volatility. This imbalance eroded trust. Rebuilding work requires redefining flexibility to include stability. Systems that combine adaptability with security are more resilient. They adjust without breaking. The choice is not between rigid protection and chaotic freedom. It is between managed flexibility and unmanaged risk.

Skills policy has been undermined by weak pathways. Training is promoted, but progression is uncertain. People invest in skills without assurance of reward. This discourages participation. Skills matter only when they lead somewhere. Britain invested in training rhetorically while neglecting demand for skilled labour. Without higher wages or advancement, skills stagnate. Rebuilding dignity requires aligning skills development with real opportunity. This means employers must commit to using and rewarding skills. Otherwise, training becomes another form of unpaid effort. Skills without pathways frustrate rather than empower.

The state plays a role as wage-setter and standard-bearer. Minimum standards, public procurement, and public-sector pay signal what work is worth. Britain often undercut itself here. Public-sector restraint depressed norms. Procurement rewarded low cost over quality. The state reinforced downward pressure. Rebuilding dignity requires leadership.

Standards must be credible and enforced. The state cannot demand dignity while modelling austerity. Its role is not to micromanage wages, but to anchor expectations. When the floor is firm, markets function better above it.

Restoring dignity at work restores meaning to contribution. People want to feel that effort matters. Fair reward reinforces belonging and trust. It signals that society values participation. When dignity is absent, compliance replaces commitment. That weakens democracy as well as the economy. Work is where most people encounter the system directly. If that encounter feels exploitative or futile, belief drains away. Rebuilding dignity is therefore political as well as economic. It underpins cohesion. Without it, reforms lack support.

The goal is not survival, but participation. An economy where work merely sustains life breeds withdrawal. An economy where work enables contribution supports renewal. Britain must choose which it wants. Rebuilding the economic base without restoring dignity will fail. Growth without fairness collapses into resentment. Dignified work is not an endpoint. It is the condition that allows people to invest in the future. The next chapters will address skills, institutions, and governance, but none of them work unless work itself once again earns security, respect, and belief.

Chapter 15 Skills, Not Just Schooling

Around 20% of UK workers are in jobs that do not use their qualifications fully.

Education in Britain expanded dramatically over recent decades. More people stayed in school longer. University attendance rose. Qualifications multiplied. Yet social mobility stalled. The promise that education would reliably deliver advancement weakened. This created confusion rather than rejection. People did what they were told: studied, qualified, complied. When outcomes disappointed, blame fell inward. Individuals assumed they chose the wrong subject, institution, or path. But when an entire generation experiences flattened returns, the issue is structural. Education continued to grow, but its connection to opportunity thinned. The system became good at producing credentials and poor at converting them into progress. This disconnect eroded faith not in learning itself, but in the bargain it was meant to represent.

Qualifications multiplied faster than opportunity. Degrees, certificates, and courses expanded, but the labour market did not absorb them proportionately. Many roles began to demand credentials that exceeded their actual requirements. This inflation did not raise productivity. It raised barriers. Credentials became filters rather than signals of capability. People invested time and money to access work that no longer rewarded that investment adequately. This conversion failure mattered. Education promised leverage. Instead, it delivered compliance. The system sorted people more finely without creating more value. When credentials cease to convert into better work or pay, they lose legitimacy. The problem is not overeducation. It is underutilisation. Britain trained people without restructuring work to use their skills.

Education and labour drifted apart. Schools and universities optimised for assessment, progression, and reputation. Employers optimised for cost control and flexibility. Feedback loops weakened. What was taught did not reliably map onto what was needed. This gap was papered over with employability rhetoric. Graduates were told to be adaptable, resilient, and entrepreneurial. This shifted responsibility onto individuals. Structural misalignment remained. Education became a sorting mechanism rather than a production system. It identified who could comply rather than what the economy required. Over time, this misalignment wasted talent. Skills decayed unused. Frustration grew. The economy lost capacity it had already paid to develop.

As credentials inflated, they excluded as much as they enabled. Jobs that once trained entrants now demanded pre-existing qualifications. Employers offloaded training costs onto individuals. This raised entry thresholds without improving performance. Skills inflation became a barrier disguised as quality control. People without credentials were locked out. People with them were underpaid. The system rewarded signalling over substance. This dynamic deepened inequality and inefficiency. Britain asked people to invest in credentials without guaranteeing return. When the price of entry rises but the prize shrinks, participation becomes cynical. People pursue education defensively rather than creatively. This undermines innovation and morale.

Training programmes proliferated, but demand for skilled labour lagged. Courses were offered. Targets were set. Uptake was encouraged. Yet many employers did not redesign jobs to use higher skills. Training without demand is wasted effort. Skills only matter when organisations change how work is done. Britain often treated skills as an individual attribute rather than a system feature. People were told to reskill into roles that did not exist or did not pay. This produced churn rather than progress. The burden of adjustment fell on workers. Employers benefited selectively. The system looked active while remaining static. Training became another form of coping.

Lifelong learning is not a slogan. It is a necessity in a changing economy. Yet Britain treated mid-career retraining as exceptional rather than normal. Support was patchy. Risk was individualised. People were expected to retrain on their own time and money, often with uncertain outcomes. This discouraged participation. Lifelong learning requires infrastructure: time, income support, clear pathways, and employer commitment. Without these, it remains aspirational. Britain praised adaptability while making it costly. This contradiction weakened capability. People cannot continuously adapt if adaptation threatens their livelihood. Making lifelong learning real requires sharing risk, not celebrating resilience.

The risk of retraining fell overwhelmingly on individuals. They bore lost income, tuition costs, and uncertainty. Employers benefited from ready-made skills without committing to development. This imbalance discouraged investment in human capital. Rational individuals avoid high-risk investments with uncertain return. Britain structured retraining as such an investment. As a result, participation skewed toward those who could afford failure. This deepened inequality. Skills policy must address risk distribution. If society needs adaptation, society must underwrite it. Leaving individuals to gamble undermines capacity. Skills systems work when risk is pooled and reward is credible.

Vocational routes and apprenticeships remained undervalued culturally and institutionally. Academic pathways were privileged. Practical skills were treated as second best. This distorted incentives and outcomes. Many productive roles require technical competence rather than abstract credentialing. Britain neglected these routes while lamenting skill shortages. Apprenticeships were rebranded repeatedly without sustained commitment. Employers hesitated. Young people received mixed signals. Rebuilding skills requires elevating vocational routes materially and symbolically. They must lead to stable, respected work. Without that, skills gaps persist regardless of policy announcements.

Skills do not exist in isolation. They develop within regional ecosystems. Training disconnected from local economic capacity fails. Britain often designed skills policy centrally, abstracted from place. This produced mismatch. People trained for jobs elsewhere or nowhere. Regional capacity must guide skills investment. This requires coordination between education, employers, and local authorities. When skills align with regional opportunity, retention improves and productivity rises. Ignoring geography wastes effort. Britain's imbalance is partly a skills mismatch. Fixing it requires anchoring learning to place.

Employers must act as educators, not just consumers of skill. Hiring finished products is insufficient in a dynamic economy. Firms that invest in development build capability and loyalty.

Britain underinvested here. Short-term labour markets discouraged training. Skills were treated as external inputs rather than internal assets. Reversing this requires incentives and expectation. Firms that benefit from skilled labour must help create it. This is not charity. It is investment. Economies that grow embed learning in work. Britain separated them. Reuniting them is essential.

Skills are not just about employability. They are about power. Capability gives people leverage, choice, and autonomy. When skills lead to better options, bargaining improves. When they do not, skills become compliance tools. Britain often framed skills as a duty rather than a resource. People were told to upskill to remain employable, not to gain control. This framing limits ambition. Skills policy must restore the link between capability and reward. Otherwise, learning feels hollow. Skills without power disappoint.

Education should enable contribution, not merely sort winners and losers. Britain's system became adept at ranking rather than building. This is inefficient and unjust. Many capable people are filtered out or underused. Rebuilding skills requires shifting purpose. Education must connect learning to meaningful work and progression. Sorting has a place. It cannot be the core function. Enabling contribution strengthens the economy and society. Britain has invested heavily in schooling. It has underinvested in conversion. Fixing that is not about more education. It is about better alignment between learning, work, and reward.

Chapter 16 Housing Is the Economy (Whether We Admit It or Not)

Mortgage lending and housing-related activity account for roughly a quarter of UK bank lending.

Housing is still discussed in Britain as if it were a social issue that happens to have economic consequences. It is framed as a matter of fairness, lifestyle, or aspiration. This framing is comforting and wrong. Housing is not a side issue. It is the economy's central constraint. Where people live determines how they work, what they earn, what risks they take, and how productive they can be. Treating housing as separate from economic policy has allowed distortions to accumulate unnoticed. The result is an economy shaped less by innovation or effort than by access to shelter. Britain continues to debate housing as if it were one policy area among many. In reality, it is the system everything else bends around. Until that is admitted plainly, reform elsewhere will keep failing for reasons that appear mysterious but are not.

The shift began when housing stopped being treated primarily as infrastructure and became an asset class. Homes were no longer just places to live. They became stores of value, vehicles for leverage, and engines of wealth accumulation. This changed incentives everywhere. Scarcity became profitable. Rising prices were celebrated. Policy began to protect value rather than expand supply. This transformation was gradual, which made it harder to challenge. Each step felt reasonable. Homeowners benefited. Governments enjoyed stability.

Credit flowed. But the logic was inverted. Instead of building to meet need, Britain learned to manage scarcity to preserve price. Once housing became an asset class, the economy reorganised itself around protecting that asset. Growth elsewhere became secondary. Housing stopped supporting the economy and began directing it.

Wages quietly adjusted to housing costs. This did not happen through formal caps or agreements. It happened through necessity. Employers knew what workers needed to survive. Workers knew what they could afford to accept. High rents and mortgages set an invisible ceiling on pay growth. Any increase was absorbed by housing rather than improving living standards. This created the illusion of stagnation without explanation. Productivity gains failed to translate into real improvement because housing captured the surplus. Pay rose on paper and stood still in practice. This mechanism operates regardless of sector or skill. It does not matter how hard people work if shelter absorbs the return. Housing becomes a tax on effort that no budget statement ever names.

Productivity depends on mobility, risk-taking, and choice. Housing undermines all three. When moving is expensive, people stay put. When rents are high, starting a business is risky. When mortgages dominate income, failure becomes unaffordable. Britain's housing costs lock people into place and behaviour. Workers cannot move to where they are most productive. Firms struggle to attract talent. Entrepreneurs hesitate. The economy becomes cautious. This is not a cultural flaw. It is a structural response to risk. Housing scarcity increases the cost of experimentation. Productivity suffers not because people lack ideas, but because they cannot afford to act on them. Housing policy quietly dictates economic behaviour.

London's housing market does not stay in London. Its gravitational pull shapes policy nationwide. Because the capital dominates political, financial, and media life, its housing pressures become national constraints. Measures that might lower prices are avoided because they would destabilise London. This caution ripples outward. Planning rules tighten everywhere. Supply lags nationally. Regions inherit prices and pressures without matching wages. The country ends up organising itself around protecting one overheated market. This distorts everything from transport investment to tax policy. London's housing market becomes a veto player. Britain does not have a national housing strategy. It has a strategy for not upsetting the capital. The consequences are paid elsewhere.

Instead of building enough homes, Britain expanded credit. Mortgages grew longer and larger. Help-to-buy schemes inflated demand. Debt replaced supply as the adjustment mechanism. This choice avoided confrontation with planning and ownership. It allowed prices to rise without shortage being addressed. Credit masked scarcity. It also deepened dependence. Households took on risk. Banks profited. Governments avoided backlash. But the underlying problem remained. Credit does not create homes. It reallocates them by ability to borrow. Britain chose leverage over construction. The result is an economy where housing access depends more on finance than function. This is fragile by design.

Planning systems became tools for managing scarcity rather than enabling growth. Restrictions were justified as protection, sustainability, or local control. Each argument had merit in isolation. Together, they constrained supply relentlessly. Development became slow, contested, and uncertain. This raised costs and discouraged investment. Scarcity became baked in. Planning ceased to be a means of shaping growth and became a mechanism for preserving value. Communities learned to defend what they had rather than accommodate what was needed. The system rewarded obstruction. Britain planned as if growth were optional. The economy absorbed the cost quietly. Productivity paid the price.

Home ownership became a political hostage. Large segments of the electorate depend on rising house prices for security. Any policy that threatens value is treated as an attack on stability. This creates paralysis. Governments know what would help supply, but cannot act without alienating voters. Housing reform becomes performative. Targets are announced. Delivery stalls. Everyone pretends to be surprised. This is not cowardice. It is structural entrapment. Once housing wealth underpins retirement, confidence, and identity, reform threatens more than markets. It threatens belief. Britain tied too much security to property. Now it cannot move without shaking itself.

Renters absorb the adjustment cost. They face instability, rising costs, and limited protection. Flexibility is demanded of them, not owners. This creates a two-speed housing system. Owners experience appreciation and security. Renters experience volatility and extraction. The economy relies on this imbalance to function. Labour market flexibility is built on housing insecurity. This is rarely acknowledged openly. Britain praises flexibility while outsourcing its cost to those without assets. This arrangement keeps wages down and mobility constrained. It also breeds resentment. Housing becomes a fault line rather than a foundation.

Housing locks advantage in time rather than effort. When you were born and when you bought matters more than what you do. This fractures the social contract. Younger generations face higher barriers with lower returns. They are told to work harder in a system that rewards earlier entry. This breeds cynicism. Housing wealth becomes inherited rather than earned. Mobility stalls. Britain's promise of progress weakens. This is not inevitable. It is the result of policy choices that privileged incumbency over access. Housing stops being a ladder and becomes a wall. The economy reflects that rigidity everywhere.

Every serious reform eventually crashes into housing. Skills initiatives fail because workers cannot relocate. Productivity strategies stall because firms cannot cluster. Immigration debates flare because housing cannot absorb growth. Public services strain because staff cannot afford to live nearby. Housing is the hidden constraint behind policy failure. Britain treats these failures as separate problems. They are not. They are expressions of the same bottleneck. Until housing supply, cost, and access are addressed directly, reforms elsewhere will disappoint. Housing determines the ceiling on everything else.

The final step is naming the constraint honestly. Housing is not a moral issue, a lifestyle choice, or a personal aspiration problem. It is economic infrastructure. When it fails, everything above it warps. Britain must stop pretending it can fix productivity, wages, or growth while protecting housing scarcity. That choice has already been made implicitly. It now needs to be confronted explicitly. Housing is the economy, whether Britain admits it or not. Until policy treats it as such, the country will continue to circle the same problems, mistaking symptoms for causes and motion for progress.

Chapter 17 Taxing Work, Protecting Wealth

Earned income can face marginal tax rates above 40%, while capital gains are often taxed at 10–20%.

Most people encounter the state first and most consistently through work. Taxes appear on payslips, deductions arrive automatically, and take-home pay quietly shrinks before it ever reaches a bank account. This shapes perception. The state feels present in effort, not in ownership. Work becomes the visible funding source for everything, from public services to debt interest. Wealth, by contrast, remains distant and abstract. Its taxation is intermittent, technical, and often invisible to those without it. This asymmetry matters. It teaches people where the burden lies. Britain's tax system makes work legible and wealth discreet. That choice frames politics and resentment. When people feel squeezed, they look to what they can see. What they cannot see feels protected. This is not accidental. It is how the system evolved, and it defines how citizens experience fairness.

Work became the easiest thing to tax for practical reasons. Employers act as collectors. Compliance is high. Income is regular and measurable. Avoidance is difficult. Governments favour certainty, and payroll taxes provide it. This convenience hardened into habit. Over time, the ease of taxing work became justification enough. Alternatives appeared complex, risky, or politically dangerous. Taxing wealth requires valuation, enforcement, and confrontation. Taxing work requires administration. Britain chose the path of least resistance. The result is a system that relies on effort as its base. When revenue needs grow, rates rise or thresholds freeze. The pressure accumulates quietly. Workers feel it immediately. The economy absorbs it slowly. Convenience becomes structure. Structure becomes destiny.

Wealth grows differently. Asset values rise without effort, often without visibility. Gains appear on balance sheets, not payslips. They are realised selectively or deferred indefinitely. This quiet growth attracts less scrutiny. It also attracts deference. Britain treats wealth accumulation as prudence rewarded rather than income earned. This framing shapes tax policy. Capital gains are lighter. Inheritance is softened. Reliefs proliferate. The justification is stability and aspiration. The effect is insulation. Wealth compounds while work circulates. This asymmetry is rarely debated openly. It persists because it is normalised. Quiet growth feels less contentious than visible deduction. The tax system reflects this comfort. It taxes motion more readily than position.

Moral stories do the work policy avoids. Income is framed as reward for effort, so taxing it feels fair. Wealth is framed as responsibility and foresight, so taxing it feels punitive. These narratives are powerful and persistent. They shape public tolerance. People accept higher taxes on wages more readily than levies on assets they hope to own one day. This aspirational logic protects incumbents. Britain's tax debate often centres on deservingness rather than impact. Who worked for what. Who saved. Who planned. These stories obscure systemic effects. Tax policy becomes a moral argument rather than an economic one. The result is stasis. Stories harden into structures. Structures resist change.

Tax reliefs accumulate like sediment. Each was justified once. Few are revisited. Reliefs for pensions, property, savings, and investment persist long after circumstances change. They narrow the base quietly. They privilege those positioned to use them. Britain rarely audits reliefs with the same scrutiny applied to spending. Forgone revenue feels less real than expenditure. This creates imbalance. The system grows complex and opaque. Work remains simple to tax. Wealth navigates exemptions. Over time, reliefs become entitlements. Removing them becomes politically equivalent to raising taxes. Governments hesitate. Complexity protects advantage. The system drifts further from neutrality with each unchanged relief.

Housing wealth sits at the centre of this protection. Property is politically sacred. It is tied to security, identity, and retirement. Taxing it directly threatens more than income. It threatens confidence. Britain avoids this confrontation. Council tax remains regressive and outdated. Land value is barely touched. Stamp duty discourages movement rather than capturing value. The result is paralysis. Housing wealth grows largely untaxed while distorting everything else. Attempts to reform are brief and cautious. The political cost is deemed too high. Housing becomes a no-go area. This choice locks the economy into imbalance. Wealth sits still. Work compensates.

Capital gains are treated more gently than labour income. Rates are lower. Allowances exist. Timing is flexible. This sends a clear signal. Returns to ownership are privileged over returns to effort. Economically, this steers behaviour. People invest in assets rather than productivity. Firms prioritise financial engineering over expansion. Individuals seek appreciation rather than innovation. Britain's productivity problem is reinforced by its tax code. When gains are rewarded more than creation, stagnation follows. This is not ideological. It is mechanical. Incentives shape outcomes. The tax system tilts the field. Growth follows the tilt.

Low-tax politics does not remove burden. It shifts it. When wealth is lightly taxed, work carries more. When reliefs narrow the base, rates rise elsewhere. Britain's tax debate often ignores this transfer. Promises of low taxes rarely specify where the load will fall. In practice, it lands on those least able to avoid it. Workers pay through frozen thresholds, reduced services, and indirect taxes. The system remains progressive on paper but regressive in effect. This fuels distrust. People feel squeezed while being told taxes are low. The contradiction erodes belief. Politics suffers. The economy adjusts downward.

The imbalance is generational. Younger workers fund systems that protect older asset holders. They pay more tax on lower real wages while facing higher housing costs. Their contributions support pensions, healthcare, and debt built under different conditions. Wealth accumulated earlier is shielded. This transfer is rarely acknowledged. It is embedded in policy. Intergenerational tension grows as outcomes diverge. Younger people see effort taxed and ownership rewarded beyond reach. This is not a moral failure of generations. It is a design choice. The tax system amplifies it. Without reform, legitimacy erodes further.

Reform stalls here because this is where power concentrates. Wealth votes. Wealth lobbies. Wealth frames debate. Complexity is used as defence. Any proposal is attacked as risky, unfair, or destructive. Governments retreat. Incremental changes are diluted. Reviews are launched. Nothing fundamental shifts. Britain knows this imbalance exists. It lacks the will to confront it. The fear is electoral. The cost is economic. Each delay deepens reliance on taxing work. The system becomes harder to unwind with time. Stalling becomes self-justifying.

The choice must be named honestly. Britain taxes effort to protect accumulated advantage. This is not a conspiracy. It is the outcome of convenience, fear, and narrative. But it is a choice. It shapes behaviour, growth, and trust. Continuing it guarantees stagnation. Changing it guarantees conflict. There is no neutral path. Pretending otherwise prolongs drift. The tax system is not just a revenue tool. It is a statement of values. Britain's current statement is clear. Whether it remains acceptable is the question that follows.

Chapter 18 Energy, Security, and Exposure

The UK imports roughly half of its energy, making it more exposed to price shocks than many peers.

Energy sits beneath everything, yet it is rarely treated as foundational. It powers homes, transport, industry, data centres, hospitals, and logistics. When it works, it disappears from attention. When it fails, everything else falters. Britain has treated energy as background infrastructure rather than a core economic system. This neglect allowed vulnerabilities to accumulate quietly. Policy focused on prices, targets, and transitions without fully grappling with dependence. Energy was assumed to be available, affordable, and stable. That assumption shaped planning across government and business. When it proved false, the shock was severe. Energy is not just another sector. It is the base layer on which productivity, security, and living standards rest. Ignoring that reality distorted decision-making for decades.

Britain planned as if cheap, reliable energy were permanent. Abundance was assumed rather than secured. Domestic production declined without replacement. Storage was neglected. Long-term contracts were allowed to lapse. The system became lean and exposed. This worked while global markets were calm. It failed under stress. The illusion of endless supply encouraged complacency. Energy policy focused on marginal efficiency rather than resilience. Short-term savings were prioritised over long-term capacity. When prices spiked, there was little buffer. Britain discovered that energy planning had been reactive rather than strategic. The consequences were immediate and widespread. Assumptions hardened into fragility. The economy paid the price.

Import dependence is not inherently bad, but unmanaged dependence is a weakness. Britain allowed its energy system to rely heavily on external suppliers without adequate safeguards. This reduced flexibility. Supply shocks became unavoidable. Decisions elsewhere began to dictate domestic outcomes. Energy exposure constrained policy. Britain's choices narrowed. Reliance on imports was treated as efficiency rather than vulnerability. It worked while conditions were benign. It failed when geopolitics shifted. Exposure is cumulative. Each dependency adds risk. Britain did not hedge adequately. The result was loss of control at moments when control mattered most. Energy became a transmission channel for external instability.

Price shocks reveal structural weakness. When energy prices surged, inflation followed. Wages lagged. Public finances strained. Businesses cut back. Energy volatility rippled through the economy. This was not a temporary inconvenience. It was a stress test. Systems designed for stability struggled under fluctuation. Britain's energy exposure amplified shocks rather than absorbing them. Households felt it quickly. Firms delayed investment. Services cut back. The economy slowed. Energy costs touched everything. This revealed how deeply energy underpins economic life. Price volatility is not just a market issue. It is a systemic risk.

Households experience energy failure directly. Bills rise. Choices narrow. Heating becomes a calculation. This makes energy policy immediate and political. People feel exposure in daily life. Britain's system transmitted wholesale instability straight into homes. There was little insulation. Support arrived late and unevenly. Trust eroded. When people cannot afford energy, the legitimacy of the system is questioned. Energy insecurity undermines confidence faster than abstract economic indicators. It brings fragility into the domestic sphere. Britain underestimated this impact. Treating energy as technical policy ignored its social consequences. Exposure became personal.

Businesses absorb energy costs quietly until they cannot. High and volatile prices suppress productivity. Firms delay expansion. Margins shrink. Investment stalls. Energy-intensive sectors struggle first, but costs cascade. Britain's competitiveness weakened. Energy costs became a silent tax on production. This discouraged manufacturing and high-value activity. Firms adapted by reducing ambition rather than innovating. Over time, this eroded capacity. Productivity suffered. Britain's energy exposure thus reinforced stagnation. The economy learned to cope rather than grow. Energy insecurity became an invisible brake on progress.

Energy policy was too often framed as environmental policy alone. Climate goals dominated discourse, while economic and security dimensions were sidelined. This narrow framing distorted priorities. Transition was treated as an end in itself rather than a means to resilience. Investment decisions became fragmented. Britain failed to integrate climate, security, and economic objectives coherently. This created gaps. Infrastructure lagged. Capacity planning suffered. Treating energy as a moral issue rather than a strategic one limited debate. The result was policy that pleased constituencies but failed systems. Energy must be understood holistically. Separating goals weakened delivery.

Infrastructure neglect was tolerated because failure was delayed. Grids aged. Storage remained limited. Maintenance lagged. These problems accumulated slowly. Because breakdown was not immediate, urgency faded. Britain deferred investment repeatedly. Short-term pressures crowded out long-term planning. When stress arrived, systems lacked resilience. Catch-up became expensive and rushed. Infrastructure failure rarely announces itself early. It reveals itself under load. Britain's energy infrastructure revealed decades of underinvestment when demand spiked. The cost of delay multiplied. Neglect proved far more expensive than preparation.

Energy policy is national security policy. Dependence limits autonomy. Exposure shapes foreign relations. Britain's energy weakness constrained its choices. Responses were shaped by vulnerability rather than strategy. Security considerations were secondary until they were unavoidable. Energy independence does not mean isolation. It means capacity to choose. Britain ceded that capacity. This affected diplomacy, defence, and domestic stability. Energy insecurity magnifies every other risk. Treating it as a technical issue left the country exposed strategically. National resilience requires energy control.

Markets alone cannot fix energy systems. Long-term infrastructure requires coordination, scale, and patience. Returns are slow. Risks are large. Britain relied heavily on market signals without sufficient direction. This produced underinvestment and fragmentation. Energy systems need planning. This does not negate markets. It complements them. Without coordination, incentives misalign. Britain's approach lacked coherence. Responsibility was diffused. Accountability weakened. Long-term outcomes suffered. Energy requires state capacity to set direction, manage risk, and ensure resilience. Abdicating that role left gaps no market could fill.

The political temptation has been to muddle through. Temporary subsidies. Short-term fixes. Crisis management. This avoids confrontation but deepens dependence. Each patch postpones reform. Exposure remains. Britain has repeatedly chosen expedience over strategy. This pattern is understandable. Energy reform is expensive and contentious. But delay compounds cost. The longer exposure persists, the narrower options become. Muddling through is itself a policy choice. It favours stability now over security later. Britain has paid for that choice repeatedly.

Britain's energy weakness magnifies every other problem. High costs worsen inflation. Exposure constrains policy. Insecurity undermines trust. Productivity suffers. Energy cannot be treated as a side issue any longer. It is a central constraint. Naming this honestly is the first step. Without confronting energy exposure directly, other reforms will falter. Britain cannot tax, build, or grow its way around energy insecurity. It must address it head-on. Energy is not just about power. It is about control. Until that is acknowledged, the country remains exposed by design.

Chapter 19 The State That Can't Deliver

The UK has fewer planners per capita than most comparable European countries.

Britain is good at promising change. Announcements come quickly. Strategies are launched. Targets are set. White papers appear. The problem is not a lack of ambition. It is that promises now routinely outrun capacity. The state commits to outcomes it no longer has the machinery to deliver. This gap has become normalised. Failure is explained away as complexity, resistance, or bad luck. Rarely is it acknowledged as a capacity problem. Over time, citizens learn to discount announcements. Reform becomes theatre. Delivery slips into the background. This is corrosive. A state that cannot reliably execute its own decisions loses authority, even when its intentions are sound. Britain's crisis of delivery is not about ideas. It is about execution.

Delivery failure is not episodic. It is patterned. Projects overrun. Programmes stall. Timelines slide. This happens across housing, transport, health, defence, and digital services. Governments change. The outcomes repeat. This repetition signals structure, not coincidence. Systems produce the results they are designed for. Britain's system now produces delay and dilution. Reviews replace action. Pilots replace scale. Responsibility shifts. Each failure is treated as unique. The accumulation is ignored. Over time, expectations adjust downward. Citizens stop expecting delivery. Institutions adapt to managing failure rather than preventing it. This is not collapse. It is drift. Drift is harder to confront because it feels survivable. Until it isn't.

The administrative core of the state has been hollowed out. Expertise drained away through outsourcing, pay restraint, and constant reorganisation. Experience became mobile. Institutional memory thinned. The state increasingly manages contracts rather than systems. This weakens its ability to design, challenge, and adapt. Skilled administrators are essential for delivery. Britain undervalued them. The result is a state that can commission but not control. Knowledge sits outside. Dependence grows. When problems arise, the state lacks the internal capacity to respond quickly. This creates fragility. Rebuilding administrative skill is slow and unglamorous. It has been deferred repeatedly. The cost is now evident.

Outsourcing was sold as efficiency. In practice, it often became avoidance. Responsibility was transferred along with risk. The state retained accountability without control. Contracts multiplied. Oversight weakened. When outcomes disappointed, blame was diffused. Outsourcing can work when the state is a strong client. Britain's state weakened as a client. It outsourced without retaining capability. This created asymmetry. Contractors learned the system. The state lost leverage. Delivery suffered. Outsourcing became default rather than strategic. It filled gaps created by hollowing out rather than complementing strength. The result is a fragmented delivery landscape where no one owns outcomes fully.

Procurement rules reward process over results. Compliance is prioritised. Risk avoidance dominates. Innovation is penalised.

Contracts are designed to prevent blame rather than ensure success. This creates perverse incentives. Suppliers focus on meeting specifications rather than solving problems. The state focuses on documentation rather than delivery. Outcomes become secondary. Britain's procurement culture reflects fear rather than ambition. It is designed to survive audits, not deliver transformation. This culture is self-reinforcing. Failure leads to more rules. More rules slow delivery further. The system protects itself rather than the public interest. This is not corruption. It is paralysis by design.

Planning delays illustrate institutional paralysis clearly. Decisions take years. Objections proliferate. Accountability diffuses. Delay becomes the safest option. Saying no invites backlash. Saying yes invites risk. Doing nothing feels neutral. It is not. Delay is a choice with costs. Britain's planning systems incentivise inertia. Projects stall. Housing is not built. Infrastructure lags. Growth is constrained. This is not because planning is unnecessary. It is because conflict resolution has been outsourced to time. Delay replaces decision. Over time, this erodes confidence. Investors hesitate. Communities stagnate. Planning becomes a brake rather than a guide.

Electoral cycles undermine delivery discipline. Long-term projects extend beyond political horizons. Incentives favour announcements over completion. Ministers move on. Priorities shift. Accountability blurs. Britain's political system rewards novelty, not follow-through. Delivery requires persistence. Systems need continuity. Politics disrupts both. This is not unique to Britain, but it is acute. The state struggles to sustain focus across terms. Each change resets momentum. Delivery suffers. Citizens experience this as incompetence. In reality, it is misaligned incentives. Without insulation for long-term delivery, systems fragment. Britain has not resolved this tension.

Responsibility is fragmented across agencies, departments, and tiers of government. No single actor owns outcomes. When things fail, everyone shares partial blame. This protects individuals but undermines delivery. Clear ownership is essential. Britain diffused it. Coordination became negotiation. Negotiation slowed action. Each layer added friction. Accountability dissolved. Citizens cannot tell who is responsible. Politicians exploit this ambiguity. The system persists because it protects itself. Fragmentation feels safer than concentration. The cost is effectiveness. Delivery requires someone to be clearly in charge. Britain resists this clarity.

The cost of delivery failure is initially invisible. Delays feel abstract. Budgets adjust. Timelines move. The impact accumulates quietly. Infrastructure decays. Services strain. Confidence erodes. When failure becomes visible, it feels sudden and severe. Britain is now experiencing this phase. What was once tolerable drift is now crisis. Catch-up costs multiply. Trust collapses faster than it can be rebuilt. Delivery failure does not announce itself early. It reveals itself late. Britain ignored early warnings. The bill is now due.

"Reform of the state" is announced regularly. It rarely sticks. Reviews recommend change. Structures are adjusted. Titles change. Underlying incentives remain. Without sustained commitment, reform dissipates. Britain treats state reform as episodic rather than continuous. This undermines impact. Real reform is slow. It requires investment, stability, and patience. It also requires admitting past mistakes. Britain avoids this discomfort. Each reform cycle promises renewal.

Each ends quietly. The state remains weakened. Cynicism deepens. Reform loses credibility.

Capacity must come before ambition. Promising more than can be delivered erodes trust further. Britain must rebuild the ability to act before expanding commitments. This requires restraint. Saying no. Setting priorities. Investing in people and systems. This is politically unattractive. It is also necessary. A state that does less but delivers it reliably regains authority. Britain inverted this logic. It promised widely and delivered narrowly. Reversing that requires discipline. Capacity is not a technical detail. It is the foundation of legitimacy.

Admitting limits is the first act of competence. Pretending otherwise prolongs failure. Britain must be honest about what its state can currently do. This is not defeatism. It is realism. From realism comes rebuilding. Without it, reform remains theatrical. Citizens are not asking for miracles. They are asking for delivery. Restoring trust begins with honesty about capacity, followed by sustained effort to rebuild it. Only then can ambition return without hollowing out belief. The state's credibility depends on closing the gap between promise and performance.

Chapter 20 The NHS: Already Rationed, Just Not Honestly

The NHS waiting list in England exceeded 7 million people in the mid-2020s.

The NHS is still described as universal and comprehensive, a service available to all, free at the point of use, based on need rather than ability to pay. This description survives because it is emotionally powerful and historically grounded. It is also increasingly untrue in practice. Access to care is uneven, delayed, and conditional. People wait months or years for treatment. Some conditions are deprioritised quietly. Others never reach a referral threshold. The language remains expansive while reality contracts. This gap is sustained by habit and fear. The NHS is treated as a moral symbol rather than a functioning system. Questioning its limits is framed as hostility. As a result, rationing exists everywhere, but nowhere officially. The system pretends to offer everything while delivering selectively. This dishonesty corrodes trust and blocks reform.

Rationing happens through delay rather than decision. Waiting lists perform the work politicians refuse to name. Care is not denied outright; it is postponed. Time becomes the filter. Those who can wait do. Those who cannot seek alternatives or deteriorate. Delay feels neutral, but it is not. It redistributes harm quietly. It allows the system to claim universality while limiting access in practice. This method avoids confrontation. No service is formally withdrawn. No explicit choices are made. The cost is invisibility. Rationing by delay obscures responsibility. It also worsens outcomes. Conditions become more complex and expensive to treat. Delay is a political convenience and a clinical failure. It keeps the myth intact while the system strains.

Honesty about limits once existed. Early debates about the NHS acknowledged scarcity. Choices were discussed openly. Over time, this candour disappeared. Medical advances expanded possibility. Expectations rose. Politicians learned that acknowledging limits was electorally dangerous. Silence replaced realism. Rationing became a dirty word. The system adapted by denying it existed. This did not remove limits. It merely hid them. Britain drifted into an arrangement where everyone knows care is constrained, but no one says so publicly. This silence is enforced culturally and politically. Clinicians understand it. Patients sense it. Politicians avoid it. The result is a system trapped between aspiration and capacity, unable to reconcile the two honestly.

Demand grew faster than any health system could absorb. Populations aged. Chronic conditions multiplied. Treatments became more sophisticated and expensive. Expectations shifted from emergency care to lifelong management. The NHS was not designed for this scale or complexity. Funding increases followed demand imperfectly. Workforce growth lagged. Infrastructure aged. None of this implies failure of intent. It reflects structural mismatch. Britain expanded what medicine could do without redefining what it would do. The gap widened gradually. The system absorbed pressure through goodwill, overtime, and delay. This masked unsustainability. Eventually, strain became visible. Demand did not suddenly spike. It accumulated. The system did not break overnight. It bent for decades.

Funding debates dominate discussion while avoiding the core issue. Arguments focus on how much money is spent rather than what is bought. Budgets rise and fall. Headlines follow. But funding alone cannot resolve mismatch without clarity on scope. Without defined limits, spending becomes reactive. Money fills gaps temporarily. Expectations remain unbounded. The cycle repeats. Britain avoids asking what level of care can be provided universally and what cannot. This avoidance makes funding debates performative. No amount of money can meet infinite demand. Pretending otherwise sets the NHS up to disappoint regardless of budget. Funding is necessary. It is not sufficient. Without scope, it becomes a proxy for honesty the system lacks.

Staff act as shock absorbers. Clinicians and nurses quietly ration care every day. They prioritise. They triage. They delay. They absorb moral injury. This rationing is informal and invisible. It relies on professionalism and sacrifice. Burnout becomes normal. Retention suffers. Workforce shortages worsen. The system depends on people smoothing over structural gaps. This is unsustainable. Staff are asked to reconcile unlimited demand with limited capacity personally. This erodes morale and quality. Rationing shifts from policy to bedside. Responsibility moves downward. When care is delayed or denied, staff carry the emotional cost. The system preserves its moral narrative by offloading reality onto individuals.

Rationing varies by location. Access depends on postcode, capacity, and local decisions. Some areas cope better than others. This creates inequality within a system that claims uniformity. Variation is inevitable to some degree. Pretending it does not exist prevents addressing it. Britain maintains a national story while living with local realities. This disconnect undermines trust. People compare experiences. Disparities become visible. The promise of equal access weakens. Postcode rationing is not new. What is new is its scale and persistence. Without honest acknowledgement, variation feels arbitrary and unjust. The system's moral authority depends on fairness. Hidden inequality erodes it quietly.

Private provision grows in the shadows. As waits lengthen, those who can pay opt out partially. This is not planned reform. It is pressure release. The private sector absorbs overflow without integration. This creates a two-tier reality beneath a one-tier story. Politicians tolerate this because it reduces visible pressure. The NHS remains symbolically intact. Inequality grows quietly. This arrangement satisfies no one fully. It undermines solidarity while avoiding honest redesign. The private system expands without accountability for system-wide outcomes. It becomes a symptom of denial rather than a solution. Britain drifts toward hybridity without admitting it has chosen one.

Pretending protects no one. Denial delays reform. It prevents honest conversation with the public. People sense reality anyway. Trust erodes when experience contradicts rhetoric. Outcomes worsen as delays compound. Resources are misallocated. Staff burn out. Patients suffer. Honesty would be painful. It would require naming trade-offs. But dishonesty is more damaging long-term. The NHS is not preserved by pretending it can do everything. It is weakened by it. A system that cannot admit limits cannot design within them. Denial traps the NHS in permanent crisis mode. Crisis management replaces planning. This is corrosive.

Other countries face similar pressures and respond differently. Many acknowledge limits explicitly. They define baskets of care. They manage demand through policy rather than delay. They maintain solidarity while recognising scarcity. Britain resists these comparisons. They feel like betrayal. The NHS is treated as unique and untouchable. This exceptionalism blocks learning. No system escapes trade-offs. Pretending Britain can is magical thinking. Comparative honesty does not mean abandoning values. It means operationalising them realistically. Refusing to learn isolates the NHS intellectually. Pride becomes a barrier to adaptation. The cost is borne by patients and staff alike.

Politicians fear naming trade-offs because they invite attack. Saying no is risky. Silence feels safer. But silence transfers risk to the system. Decisions still happen, just informally and unevenly. Accountability dissolves. The public is treated as incapable of understanding limits. This is a misjudgement. People accept difficult truths when they are explained honestly and fairly. What they resent is being misled. Avoiding trade-offs infantilises debate. It undermines democratic consent. The NHS is sustained by public trust. That trust depends on honesty. Political fear has produced systemic dishonesty. The result is a service drifting without direction.

Truth is the only route to preservation. Admitting rationing does not destroy the NHS. It gives it a chance to adapt deliberately. Scope can be defined. Priorities can be debated. Resources can be aligned. Staff can be supported honestly. Patients can make informed choices. None of this is easy. All of it is necessary. The alternative is continued erosion under a false narrative. The NHS will not collapse suddenly. It will hollow out gradually. Preserving it requires confronting reality, not denying it. Honesty is not abandonment. It is stewardship. Only by naming limits can the NHS remain worthy of the loyalty it still commands.

Chapter 21 Why No Government Will Fix This Properly

....

Every government campaigns on fixing what is broken. It promises renewal, competence, and relief. Once in office, it inherits constraints it cannot easily name. Structural problems are acknowledged privately and avoided publicly. The gap between rhetoric and reality opens immediately. Governments fear admitting limits because elections reward optimism and punish restraint. Promises become traps. They must be maintained even as evidence accumulates that delivery will fall short. Retreat feels like betrayal. Escalation feels reckless. So governments manage perception instead of substance. They adjust language, announce reviews, and buy time. This is not cynicism. It is survival. The system selects for leaders who avoid pain. Fixing deep problems requires imposing it. The promise trap ensures most governments never try.

Electoral cycles collide with structural timelines. Problems built over decades cannot be fixed in one term. Benefits arrive slowly. Costs arrive quickly. Voters experience disruption before improvement. Governments face elections before results. This misalignment shapes behaviour. Policies are chosen for immediate visibility rather than long-term impact. Maintenance is neglected. Investment is deferred. Announcements replace follow-through. Structural reform requires continuity across administrations. Britain's politics struggles to provide it. Each election resets priorities. Long-term projects lose protection. Governments rationally prioritise survival. The system rewards short-termism even when leaders understand its damage. Fixing this requires insulating delivery from electoral churn. Britain has not done so. The cycle repeats predictably.

Blame avoidance becomes strategy. When reform threatens backlash, responsibility is diffused. Decisions are delayed. Committees are formed. Consultations extend. Failures are attributed to complexity or circumstance. Ownership is avoided. This is rational behaviour in a hostile environment. Politicians who own pain become targets. Those who defer it survive. Over time, systems adapt to minimise blame rather than maximise outcomes. Britain's governance reflects this. Hard choices are postponed. Soft language replaces decision. Blame avoidance does not remove costs. It shifts them forward. Future governments inherit larger problems. Each round of avoidance narrows options further. The system selects for evasion. Results deteriorate.

Reforms fail when costs are immediate and visible while benefits are delayed or diffuse. Housing reform angers owners now and helps renters later. Tax reform creates losers quickly and gains slowly. Energy reform raises bills before stabilising supply. Politicians face voters now. Future beneficiaries are abstract. This asymmetry is decisive. Governments know this. They retreat. Even popular reforms die when opposition mobilises faster than support. Britain's politics amplifies this dynamic. Vocal minorities exert pressure. Quiet majorities adapt silently. Visible losers dominate headlines. Benefits remain hypothetical. Governments respond accordingly. Reform becomes politically irrational even when economically necessary. The system favours stasis.

Voters are not idealists. They are risk managers. They value stability, predictability, and personal security. When faced with uncertain reform, they hesitate. They punish perceived recklessness. Governments misread this as conservatism. It is pragmatism. People living near the margin cannot absorb shocks easily. Reform threatens that balance. Even those who agree in principle resist in practice. This creates a paradox. Demand for change coexists with fear of disruption. Politicians navigate this tension by promising change without specifying cost. Once costs emerge, support evaporates. Governments learn to avoid the confrontation entirely. The cycle deepens distrust. Voters sense evasion. Politicians sense danger. Nothing moves.

Opposition parties are incentivised to oppose. Supporting difficult reform risks sharing blame without credit. Adversarial politics rewards attack over continuity. Even sensible policies become targets when they originate elsewhere. Britain's system intensifies this. Cooperation is framed as weakness. Compromise is punished. Long-term projects require cross-party support. It rarely arrives. Governments act alone and reverse course when power shifts. Institutional memory erodes. Delivery suffers. Each administration dismantles what the last built. Reform becomes episodic and fragile. The system discourages shared ownership of difficult choices. Without it, no government wants to move first. Stalemate follows.

Media cycles flatten complexity. Trade-offs become scandals. Nuance disappears. Policy is judged by headline rather than outcome. Governments adapt by simplifying messages and avoiding detail. This rewards slogans over substance. Britain's media environment accelerates this pressure. Social media amplifies outrage. Explanations are drowned out. Politicians retreat into defensiveness. Honest discussion becomes risky. Reform requires explaining why some things must change and others cannot. This explanation rarely survives the cycle intact. Governments learn to minimise exposure. Complexity is hidden. Decisions are softened. The public receives fragments. Trust erodes further. The system selects for superficiality.

The myth of the decisive moment persists. Governments wait for crises to force action. They hope necessity will override resistance. Sometimes it does. Often it narrows options instead. Crisis compresses time. Decisions are rushed. Trade-offs are harsher. Public consent is thinner. Britain's experience shows this repeatedly. Waiting for crisis does not make reform easier. It makes it uglier. Yet governments delay anyway. The decisive moment feels external and unavoidable. Acting early feels elective and risky. This bias toward delay compounds damage. By the time action is unavoidable, options are constrained. Outcomes worsen. The myth persists because it absolves responsibility.

Policy churn exhausts institutions. Constant reform announcements disrupt delivery. Staff adapt to new priorities before completing old ones. Systems never stabilise. Learning is lost. Britain's state experiences reform fatigue. Each government announces transformation. Few see it through. Capacity erodes. Cynicism grows. Institutions learn to wait out initiatives. This undermines effectiveness. Real reform requires patience and continuity. Britain offers neither consistently. Churn replaces consolidation. The appearance of action substitutes for impact. Governments measure activity rather than results. The system deteriorates quietly. Exhaustion replaces ambition.

Inherited excuses comfort governments. Blaming predecessors deflects accountability. It explains failure without requiring change. Britain's politics normalises this. Each administration inherits problems and promises correction. When correction fails, blame shifts backward. Patterns repeat. The public grows weary. Excuses lose credibility. Yet the habit persists. Owning structural failure requires acknowledging continuity across governments. That admission undermines partisan narratives. Politicians avoid it. The result is perpetual restart. No one owns the long arc. Problems deepen. Excuses multiply. Trust thins.

Competence increasingly looks like caution. Leaders who move slowly and avoid disruption are labelled weak. Those who promise bold change gain attention. This reverses incentives. Sensible restraint is punished. Reckless ambition is rewarded rhetorically. Governments respond by promising more than they can deliver. When delivery falters, cynicism grows. Britain's politics confuses seriousness with spectacle. Competence requires saying no. Politics punishes it. The system therefore selects for performative strength rather than effective governance. Reform becomes theatre. Delivery remains elusive.

Understanding why governments fail does not mean surrender. It clarifies constraints. Systems must be designed to reduce reliance on heroics. Long-term delivery requires insulation from electoral cycles, shared ownership of pain, and honest communication. Britain lacks these protections. Expecting individual governments to overcome structural incentives is unrealistic. Reform requires changing the environment governments operate within. Without that, each administration will repeat the same pattern. Naming this is not defeatism. It is realism. Only by acknowledging the limits of politics can Britain design institutions capable of doing what politics alone cannot.

Chapter 22 The Reforms Everyone Agrees On (And Still Won't Do)

Housebuilding has consistently fallen short of official targets by tens of thousands of homes per year.

Britain does not lack agreement about what is wrong. On housing, tax, pensions, energy, skills, and public services, there is broad consensus across politics, business, and the media. Reports pile up. Think tanks align. Speeches echo each other. The problem is not diagnosis. It is consequence. Agreement creates the illusion of progress without the reality of change. When everyone agrees, no one feels urgency. Consensus becomes a resting place rather than a launch point. Reform is acknowledged, logged, and postponed. This produces a peculiar stagnation. Britain knows what needs doing and behaves as if knowing were sufficient. Agreement substitutes for action. The country circles familiar problems, reassured by recognition while avoiding disruption. This is not ignorance. It is avoidance wearing the mask of wisdom.

Planning reform is the clearest example. Almost everyone agrees Britain needs to build more homes. Shortages are obvious. Prices signal scarcity relentlessly. Yet delivery stalls. The agreement is abstract and conditional. People support building in principle and oppose it in practice. Politicians endorse reform nationally and retreat locally. The system absorbs this contradiction. Targets are announced and missed. Blame shifts. No one is surprised. Consensus provides cover. Because everyone agrees housing is broken, no one is forced to act decisively. Responsibility diffuses. Reform becomes performative. Britain demonstrates awareness while preserving scarcity. Agreement without enforcement becomes a mechanism for stasis. Housing remains constrained because agreement never confronts cost.

Pensions arithmetic is similarly uncontested. Demographics are clear. People live longer. Fewer workers support more retirees. Contributions and payouts no longer align sustainably. This is acknowledged quietly across parties. Yet reform is endlessly deferred. Pensions are treated as untouchable promises rather than adjustable systems. Agreement exists on the maths, not on the response. Politicians fear backlash. Voters fear loss. The result is paralysis. Adjustments that could be gradual become sudden later. Consensus enables delay. Everyone knows change is coming. No one wants to own it. The longer reform is postponed, the harsher it becomes. Agreement without action stores up future conflict. Britain chooses postponement repeatedly.

Tax reform occupies the same space. Economists agree the system is inefficient and distorting. It taxes work heavily and wealth lightly. It narrows the base and complicates compliance. This is not controversial in expert circles. Yet reform is avoided. Each proposal triggers resistance from affected groups. Agreement dissolves when specifics appear. Governments revert to tweaks. Reliefs remain. Thresholds freeze. Structural imbalance persists. The consensus is broad but shallow. It survives only while abstract. When choices are named, unity evaporates. Tax reform becomes a theoretical exercise. Britain lives with a system everyone criticises and no one changes. Agreement becomes an alibi.

Skills and training are perennial priorities. Every strategy emphasises them. Every government announces initiatives. Yet outcomes disappoint. The agreement is rhetorical. Skills are treated as universally beneficial without confronting demand. Employers endorse training while resisting higher wages. Governments fund courses without restructuring work. The same reforms are recycled. Apprenticeships are relaunched. Lifelong learning is praised. Structural alignment is avoided. Agreement allows repetition without progress. The system moves but does not advance. Skills policy becomes ritual. Britain mistakes activity for effectiveness. Consensus sustains motion without direction. The result is frustration rather than transformation.

Energy policy also suffers from agreed ambition and disputed cost. Everyone supports resilience, affordability, and transition. Disagreement emerges over sequencing and burden. Costs are deferred. Trade-offs are obscured. Agreement exists on goals, not on means. This encourages delay. Governments announce targets without building capacity. Infrastructure lags. Exposure remains. Consensus on aspiration substitutes for commitment to delivery. Energy policy becomes symbolic. Britain reassures itself with agreement while remaining vulnerable. When shocks arrive, surprise is feigned. The gap between ambition and capacity persists. Agreement delays reckoning.

Public services illustrate consensus without redesign. Everyone agrees services are under strain. Funding debates dominate. Structural questions are avoided. How services are delivered, prioritised, and evaluated remains largely unchanged. Reform is framed as rescue rather than redesign. This preserves existing models even as demand overwhelms them. Agreement on strain produces funding injections without systemic change. The cycle repeats. Services lurch from crisis to crisis. Britain treats reform as temporary relief. Consensus avoids confrontation with scope and expectation. The system survives but does not improve. Agreement becomes a brake on rethinking.

Agreement can make action harder. When everyone nods, urgency fades. No one owns the problem. Leadership dissipates. Reform requires someone to push against resistance. Consensus removes that impetus. Opposition is muted but not absent. It reappears when action threatens interests. By then, momentum is gone. Britain's political culture rewards harmony over decision. Agreement feels like achievement. It is not. Without ownership, reform stalls. Consensus becomes a comfort blanket. It reassures elites while frustrating outcomes. Action requires friction. Agreement removes it prematurely.

Distributed pain undermines reform. When costs are spread thinly, opposition is diffuse but persistent. Each group resists its share. No coalition forms to support change. Benefits are collective and delayed. Costs are individual and immediate. Agreement masks this asymmetry. People support reform until it affects them. Governments retreat. Britain struggles to design reforms that concentrate pain or compensate losers explicitly. Distributed pain feels fair but is politically lethal. Consensus hides this dynamic. Reform collapses under its own even-handedness.

Consultation becomes displacement activity. Reviews, commissions, and inquiries proliferate. They signal seriousness without forcing decisions. Stakeholders are engaged. Time passes. Momentum dissipates. Consultation substitutes for commitment. Britain excels at this. It produces excellent analysis and little change. Agreement fuels this cycle. Because diagnosis is shared, further consultation seems prudent. In reality, it delays action. Each review refreshes the consensus without altering incentives. Reform remains perpetually imminent. This creates fatigue. People disengage. The system settles into managed inertia.

Timing is blamed repeatedly. Reform is said to be right but poorly timed. After elections. After crises. After growth returns. Timing becomes the excuse that never expires. Agreement supports this deferral. Everyone agrees reform is necessary, just not now. Britain waits for a moment when reform is painless. It never arrives. Delaying action makes it harder. Options narrow. Costs rise. Agreement becomes a promise to future governments that is never redeemed. Timing is not the issue. Willingness is.

Agreement can be a sophisticated form of avoidance. By sharing diagnosis, Britain avoids decision. By acknowledging problems, it defers responsibility. Consensus becomes a way of not acting while appearing serious. This is more dangerous than denial. Denial invites challenge. Consensus disarms it. The country drifts while congratulating itself on awareness. Reform requires moving from agreement to imposition. Someone must decide. Someone must accept blame. Until that happens, Britain will continue to live with problems everyone recognises and no one resolves.

Chapter 23 Immigration as a Pressure Valve, Not a Plan

Net migration has exceeded 500,000 per year while housing supply has not kept pace.

Immigration has become Britain's default pressure valve. When labour shortages appear, migration expands. When growth falters, inflows rise. When services strain, the adjustment is absorbed quietly. Immigration is treated as a flexible input rather than a strategic choice. This approach relieves immediate pressure without addressing root causes. It keeps systems functioning just enough to avoid collapse. That makes it politically attractive. It also makes it evasive. Immigration substitutes for reform. It delays decisions on pay, training, housing, and productivity. Britain uses migration to stabilise outcomes while leaving structures intact. This is not inherently hostile to migration. It is a critique of avoidance. Immigration becomes a tool for managing symptoms rather than solving problems. Over time, the valve is opened wider. Pressure returns. The cycle repeats.

Headline growth figures look healthier than lived reality. Population growth boosts aggregate GDP. Output rises. The economy appears to expand. Per-capita gains tell a different story. Productivity remains weak. Wages stagnate. Living standards barely move. Immigration props up totals without transforming fundamentals. This disconnect fuels confusion. Politicians cite growth. People feel stuck. Both are true. Immigration increases economic activity while diluting its impact per person. Britain relies on this arithmetic. It flatters performance while masking stagnation. Growth without improvement becomes normal. This erodes trust. People experience decline while being told the economy is growing. Immigration is not the cause of stagnation, but it is used to disguise it. The valve releases pressure without fixing the pipe.

Labour shortages are filled, not solved. Migration supplies workers to sectors with low pay, poor conditions, and limited progression. This stabilises output but entrenches problems. Employers meet demand without changing incentives. Wages remain low. Training is deferred. Productivity improvements are unnecessary. Migration absorbs dysfunction. Britain avoids confronting why roles cannot be filled domestically. The answer is rarely skills alone. It is often pay, conditions, and housing costs. Immigration allows these issues to persist. It is easier to recruit than reform. This is rational behaviour for firms. It is damaging for the system. Labour supply expands. Structural weakness remains. The shortage returns.

Employers often prefer supply expansion to reform. Redesigning work is costly and risky. Raising wages compresses margins. Investing in productivity takes time. Recruiting from a global labour pool is faster. Britain's policy environment encourages this choice. Migration becomes the path of least resistance. Firms adapt rationally. The economy adapts poorly. Productivity lags. Skills development stalls. Britain becomes dependent on continuous inflow to sustain output. This dependence grows quietly. Employers plan around it. Policy reinforces it. Reform is postponed. Immigration becomes structural, not complementary. The system adjusts downward in ambition.

Public services absorb the strain. Housing, healthcare, education, and transport adjust to population growth without proportional investment. This is rarely acknowledged honestly. Migration increases demand. Capacity lags. Services stretch. Waiting lists grow. Class sizes rise. Housing shortages intensify. These pressures are distributed unevenly. Some areas cope better. Others struggle. Immigration is blamed publicly. Policy choices are hidden. Britain avoids matching inflows with infrastructure. The valve releases economic pressure while transferring social cost. This fuels resentment. Services feel overwhelmed. Communities feel ignored. The issue is not migration itself. It is unmanaged adjustment. Without planning, pressure concentrates. Trust erodes.

Immigration creates the illusion of dynamism. Cities feel busier. Labour markets churn. Consumption rises. This movement is mistaken for progress. Structural indicators remain unchanged. Productivity does not improve. Investment does not surge. Skills systems do not transform. Immigration creates motion without direction. Britain confuses activity with advancement. This misreading delays reform. The economy appears alive. Underneath, capacity stagnates. Immigration masks inertia. It buys time. Time is not used well. The illusion persists until pressure overwhelms it. Then migration is blamed for failures it was used to conceal.

Immigration is politically convenient. It allows governments to avoid confronting domestic trade-offs. Low pay can persist. Housing reform can be delayed. Training can be underfunded. Migration fills gaps. Moral arguments are deployed selectively. Immigration is framed as inevitable or virtuous. Critique is stigmatised. This shuts down honest discussion. Immigration policy becomes a proxy battleground. Underlying choices remain untouched. Britain outsources difficult decisions.

Migration carries the burden. When tensions rise, politics polarises. The original avoidance remains unexamined. Immigration becomes both solution and scapegoat. This dynamic is corrosive.

Distributional effects are rarely discussed openly. Some benefit. Employers gain flexibility. Consumers enjoy lower prices. Some workers face competition. Some communities absorb rapid change. Costs and benefits are uneven. Britain prefers national narratives to local reality. This silence breeds mistrust. People experience pressure without explanation. Immigration debates become distorted. Legitimate concerns are dismissed or exaggerated. Without honest accounting, policy fails to adapt. Immigration is treated as uniformly beneficial or harmful. Reality is mixed. Acknowledging distributional effects would require targeted policy. Britain avoids this complexity. The valve remains blunt.

Immigration cannot fix productivity alone. Output per worker depends on capital, technology, and organisation. More workers increase output, not efficiency. Britain relies on labour expansion to sustain growth. Productivity stagnates. This is not inevitable. Immigration can complement reform. Without reform, it substitutes for it. Britain chose substitution. The result is an economy that grows by adding people rather than improving systems. This approach has limits. Infrastructure strains. Services buckle. Wages stall. Productivity remains weak. Immigration delays reckoning. It does not remove it.

Social cohesion strains under unmanaged pressure. Rapid change without planning unsettles communities. Housing tightens. Services strain. Cultural adjustment is uneven. This is not a failure of tolerance. It is a failure of preparation. Britain allowed population growth without matching investment. People adapt as best they can. Trust frays. Immigration becomes politicised. Blame shifts. The original policy failure remains obscured. Cohesion requires planning and honesty. Britain provided neither consistently. Pressure accumulated. Debate polarised. The valve releases pressure in one place and builds it in another.

The debate is framed falsely as openness versus control. This blocks sensible policy. Immigration can be both open and managed. It can support growth without substituting for reform. Britain avoids this middle ground. Extremes dominate discourse. Policy oscillates. Uncertainty persists. Employers and communities adapt defensively. A functional system would align immigration with housing, services, and productivity goals. Britain has not done this. The false choice persists because it avoids trade-offs. Immigration remains a pressure valve, not a plan.

Immigration should be a complement, not a substitute. It can enhance growth when paired with reform. It can fill genuine gaps. It cannot replace investment, training, or productivity improvement. Britain used it to avoid these harder tasks. This strategy worked temporarily. Its costs are now visible. Continuing will deepen strain. Ending it abruptly would cause shock. The answer is integration, not denial. Immigration policy must be designed alongside domestic reform. Until then, Britain will continue to rely on the valve while the system beneath remains unrepaired.

Chapter 24 Waiting for Growth That Isn't Coming

UK economic growth has averaged under 1.5% per year since the financial crisis.

Growth has become Britain's universal escape hatch. When problems feel too difficult, growth is invoked as the solution that will arrive later. Higher wages will come with growth. Better services will come with growth. Lower taxes will be possible once growth returns. This assumption allows postponement. It makes trade-offs seem temporary rather than structural. Growth is treated as a force of nature rather than an outcome of conditions. Britain waits for it as if it were weather. This waiting shapes policy. Hard choices are deferred. Costs are pushed forward. Present discomfort is justified by future abundance. Growth becomes the promise that resolves contradiction without requiring decision. When growth does not arrive, the promise is renewed rather than questioned. Waiting becomes policy.

The promise of growth is always imminent. Forecasts predict recovery just ahead. Next year will be better. The year after will deliver momentum. Each cycle resets expectation. When outcomes disappoint, explanations multiply. External shocks are blamed. Underlying assumptions remain intact. Growth is never abandoned as a narrative. It is rescheduled. Britain's politics relies on this elasticity. Leaders avoid saying growth will be lower than hoped. They promise acceleration instead. This maintains optimism while avoiding adjustment. The gap between promise and reality widens. People experience stagnation while hearing anticipation. Trust erodes slowly. Growth talk becomes ritual rather than plan. The country waits, reassured and frustrated at the same time.

Post-war growth remains the reference point. Britain measures itself against decades of rapid expansion driven by reconstruction, demographics, and global integration. Those conditions no longer apply. Yet expectations persist. Policy debates assume similar headroom exists. This creates disappointment. Modern economies grow more slowly. Productivity gains are harder. Demographic tailwinds have turned to headwinds. Britain clings to an outdated benchmark. When growth underperforms, it feels like failure rather than normality. This distorts choices. Governments chase acceleration rather than adaptation. They design policy for a past that will not return. Waiting for familiar growth becomes a way of avoiding acceptance. Reality is postponed.

Productivity flatlines are hidden by optimism. Forecasts assume improvement. Plans depend on it. When productivity fails to rise, explanations focus on temporary factors. Structural weakness is downplayed. Britain has lived with low productivity growth for years. Yet policy continues to assume reversal. This optimism sustains waiting. Investment decisions are delayed. Reforms are softened. The expectation of future productivity gains reduces urgency to act now. When gains do not materialise, disappointment accumulates. The economy adjusts downward quietly. Productivity is not a mystery. It reflects investment, skills, and organisation. Waiting for it to rise without changing conditions is magical thinking. Britain indulges it repeatedly.

Demographics work against expansion. Ageing populations reduce labour supply growth. Dependency ratios rise. More output is required to maintain living standards. This reality constrains growth potential. Britain acknowledges demographics in reports and ignores them in policy. Growth assumptions remain unchanged. This disconnect matters. Policies designed for expansion struggle under contraction. Public finances strain. Services face pressure. Waiting for growth ignores demographic arithmetic. Adjusting to it requires difficult choices about work, retirement, and spending. Growth narratives allow avoidance. Britain waits for expansion to offset ageing. It will not. Demography is slow, predictable, and unforgiving. Ignoring it compounds difficulty.

Debt has been used to simulate growth. Borrowing supports spending. Activity is sustained. The appearance of momentum is created. This works temporarily. It does not build capacity. Debt pulls demand forward. It does not increase long-term output. Britain relied on this mechanism repeatedly. When growth disappointed, borrowing filled gaps. This delayed adjustment. It also increased vulnerability. Debt service consumes resources. Fiscal space narrows. Each cycle leaves less room. Growth is expected to rescue balance sheets later. This hope sustains borrowing. When growth underperforms, the cycle tightens. Waiting for growth becomes dependency on it. Debt substitutes for strategy.

Investment underperforms despite low interest rates and high need. Uncertainty deters capital. Planning delays stall projects. Returns appear weak. Britain struggles to convert opportunity into commitment. Growth assumptions paper over this. Governments expect private investment to surge once confidence returns. Confidence depends on clarity and delivery. Britain provides neither consistently. Investors wait. Government waits. Growth is expected to bridge the gap. It does not. Underinvestment persists. Capacity stagnates. Waiting becomes mutual. Everyone anticipates movement that requires someone else to act first. Growth is blamed for not arriving. The conditions for it remain unchanged.

Innovation exists without diffusion. Britain produces ideas, research, and start-ups. Scaling is rare. Productivity gains fail to spread. This limits growth impact. Waiting for innovation to transform the economy ignores the diffusion problem. Innovation alone is insufficient. It must be adopted, integrated, and scaled. Britain's structures inhibit this. Fragmented markets, weak coordination, and risk aversion slow spread. Growth forecasts assume diffusion will improve naturally. It has not. The economy remains uneven. Islands of excellence coexist with stagnation. Waiting for innovation to rescue growth avoids confronting structural barriers. The result is disappointment rather than transformation.

Global growth is slower than before. Britain operates within this context. Export markets expand less rapidly. Competition intensifies. Trade no longer delivers easy gains. Britain prefers to ignore this. Growth narratives assume favourable external conditions. When they fail, blame shifts. The world has changed. Growth is harder everywhere. Britain's challenges are not unique. Pretending otherwise inflates expectations. Policy is designed for conditions that no longer exist. Waiting for global growth to lift all boats is unrealistic. The tide is lower. Boats scrape. Adjusting to this reality requires redesign. Waiting preserves illusion.

Forecasts provide political shelter. They justify delay. If growth is coming, reform can wait. Projections fill speeches and budgets. When forecasts are wrong, they are revised quietly. Accountability fades. Growth forecasts become instruments of hope rather than planning. Britain relies on them heavily. This reliance reduces urgency. Decisions are postponed until conditions improve. Conditions do not. Waiting becomes habitual. Forecasts replace strategy. This undermines credibility. People notice the gap. Growth is always next year. Reality is now. The shelter collapses slowly.

Waiting too long is dangerous. Options narrow. Costs rise. Adjustment becomes harsher. Britain's habit of waiting for growth has increased fragility. Problems compound. Debt rises. Services strain. Trust erodes. Growth, when it arrives, cannot undo accumulated damage. The longer adjustment is postponed, the more painful it becomes. Waiting feels safe. It is not. It is a decision with consequences. Britain has chosen it repeatedly. Each choice makes the next harder. The danger is not low growth alone. It is denial of it.

Choosing adjustment over illusion is unavoidable. Britain must plan for a world of lower growth and adapt accordingly. This does not mean surrender. It means realism. Policy must work under constrained conditions. Services must be designed for demand that outpaces resources. Living standards must be stabilised without fantasy. Growth, if it comes, becomes upside rather than rescue. Waiting for it to solve contradictions has failed. Adjustment is not defeatism. It is preparation. Britain can manage decline or stumble into shock. The choice is not between growth and adjustment. It is between honesty and delay.

Chapter 25 Managed Decline vs Sudden Shock

Living standards in the UK stagnated for longer after 2008 than in most advanced economies.

Nations that lose momentum tend to drift into one of two paths. The first is managed decline: a slow adjustment to reduced capacity, lower ambition, and diminished expectations. The second is sudden shock: an abrupt rupture triggered by crisis, exposure, or loss of confidence. What does not exist is a third path where decline is avoided without change. Britain often behaves as if such a path exists. It assumes continuity without cost. This assumption is dangerous. Decline is not optional once underlying conditions shift. The choice lies in how it is experienced. Gradual adjustment spreads pain over time. Sudden shock concentrates it. Pretending there is an escape route delays preparation. It increases vulnerability. The absence of crisis is mistaken for success. In reality, it is often just a lull before consequence. Britain's position must be understood in these terms. The question is not whether adjustment will occur, but how.

Managed decline operates quietly. Living standards slip incrementally. Services become thinner. Infrastructure ages. Ambition narrows. None of this feels dramatic in isolation. Each year looks much like the last, just slightly worse. People adapt. Expectations recalibrate downward. Politics adjusts. Promises become smaller. This process can be stable for long periods. It feels survivable. It avoids panic. It preserves social order. Managed decline is not collapse. It is erosion. It relies on buffers: savings, trust, institutional strength. These buffers absorb loss gradually. The danger lies in mistaking endurance for resilience. Managed decline works until buffers thin. When they do, the system becomes brittle. What once felt controlled can accelerate unexpectedly. Drift masks fragility. That is its risk.

Britain shows clear signs of having chosen drift. Problems are acknowledged but postponed. Adjustments are incremental. Cuts are spread thinly. Reliance on goodwill is high. Institutions cope rather than transform. This approach avoids confrontation. It keeps politics manageable. It also entrenches decline. Each year of delay reduces capacity to reverse course. Choices narrow. Ambition shrinks. Britain is not collapsing. It is adjusting quietly to less. This adjustment is rarely named. It happens through lowered expectations rather than explicit decisions. Drift feels pragmatic. It is also cumulative. Once a society normalises decline, reversing it becomes harder. Britain's current trajectory reflects preference for tolerable loss over disruptive change.

Buffers have absorbed pressure for years. Household savings. Institutional credibility. Professional commitment. Social trust. These resources are finite. They thin quietly. Because they are intangible, their depletion is hard to measure. Britain relies heavily on them. Staff compensate for system failure. Communities absorb strain. Markets extend patience. This cannot continue indefinitely. Buffers erode faster under repeated stress. Once depleted, systems respond differently. Small shocks produce large reactions. Confidence breaks. Britain's buffers are not gone. They are thinner. Ignoring this increases risk. Managed decline depends on buffers remaining intact. When they weaken, drift gives way to instability. The transition can be rapid. What looked like control reveals itself as fragility.

Sudden shock occurs when weakened systems face stress they can no longer absorb. External events like energy crises, financial instability, or geopolitical conflict can trigger it. Internal failures can do the same. Shock feels abrupt because the buildup was ignored. In reality, it is the culmination of accumulated weakness. Systems designed to cope gradually fail suddenly. Britain is exposed to such triggers. Dependence, debt, and thin capacity increase risk. Shock is not inevitable. It is conditional. It becomes more likely as drift continues. Each postponed reform increases exposure. Shock compresses time. Decisions must be made quickly under pressure. Options are limited. Costs are higher. The social and political consequences are severe.

Shocks feel sudden because their causes were dispersed over time. Warning signs were present. They were rationalised away. Managed decline normalises underperformance. When crisis hits, it appears disproportionate. In reality, it reveals reality abruptly. Britain's institutions are accustomed to coping. They are less prepared for rupture. Shock overwhelms coping mechanisms. Trust erodes rapidly. Markets react. Politics polarises. The same problems that were tolerated gradually become intolerable at once. This dynamic explains why shocks feel surprising even when they are predictable. Drift dulls attention. Shock restores it brutally.

Under drift, pain is distributed unevenly and quietly. Some lose more than others. Inequality widens. Decline is absorbed by those with least power. Cuts are small but persistent. No single moment triggers outrage. This allows decline to proceed without mobilisation. People adapt individually rather than collectively. Politics reflects this fragmentation. Anger is diffuse. Protest is limited. Drift preserves order at the cost of fairness. Britain exhibits this pattern. Loss is normalised. Resentment simmers. Because pain is not concentrated, it does not force change. Managed decline is politically stable until it isn't.

Under shock, pain is concentrated and visible. Systems fail quickly. Losses are sudden. People react collectively. Anger escalates. Politics destabilises. Emergency measures follow. Shock produces clarity but little control. Decisions are rushed. Mistakes multiply. The distribution of pain is blunt. Some are protected. Others are devastated. Social cohesion is tested severely. Britain's institutions are not designed for shock. They rely on gradualism. A sudden rupture would strain them. The appeal of drift lies in avoiding this scenario. The danger is that drift increases the likelihood of shock by weakening resilience over time.

Political responses differ under drift and crisis. Drift produces cynicism. Trust erodes slowly. Participation declines. Politics becomes managerial and performative. Crisis produces panic. Authority is centralised. Freedoms are constrained. Decisions bypass process. Britain's politics has adapted to drift. It struggles with crisis. This is not a judgement of intent. It is structural. Systems optimised for stability are poor at adaptation under pressure. Choosing drift avoids crisis politics. It also avoids renewal. The longer drift continues, the harsher crisis politics becomes if shock arrives. This trade-off is rarely discussed openly.

Countries prefer drift because it feels humane. It avoids trauma. It preserves routines. It spreads pain. It maintains legitimacy for longer. Leaders prefer it because it reduces immediate risk. Voters tolerate it because it is familiar. Drift feels controllable. Shock does not. This preference explains Britain's choices. Gradual loss is chosen over decisive change. This is understandable. It is also risky. Drift consumes options slowly. When choice disappears, shock chooses for you. Preference for drift is rational in the short term and dangerous in the long term. Britain must recognise this trade-off explicitly.

Calm is often mistaken for stability. The absence of crisis is taken as proof that systems work. This misreading sustains drift. Britain experiences calm punctuated by manageable stress. This is interpreted as resilience. In reality, it may reflect unused buffers. Stability is not the absence of failure. It is the presence of capacity to respond. Britain's capacity has been thinning. Calm may simply indicate that stress has not yet exceeded tolerance. Mistaking calm for success delays action. When calm breaks, the adjustment is harsher. Recognising this distinction is crucial.

The real choice is not decline versus prosperity. That framing is misleading. The choice is between controlled adjustment and uncontrolled shock. Managed decline can be shaped. It can be made fairer. It can preserve capacity. Shock cannot. Britain must decide whether to manage adjustment deliberately or continue drifting until choice is removed. This requires honesty about limits and priorities. It requires acting before crisis forces action. Decline does not have to mean collapse. It does require acceptance and design. The worst outcome is not lower growth. It is loss of control. Britain still has agency. That agency narrows with time.

Chapter 26 Britain's Real Position in the World

UK GDP per capita now sits below that of several smaller European economies.

Britain is often described in extremes. Either it is still a major global power, punching above its weight, shaping events through history, alliances, and expertise. Or it is dismissed as irrelevant, a former empire clinging to nostalgia. Both descriptions are wrong. Britain sits between power and irrelevance. It still matters, but not in the way it once did and not in the way it sometimes claims. This in-between position is uncomfortable. It resists slogans. It requires nuance. Britain is neither dominant nor marginal. It has influence without command. It participates without controlling outcomes. Accepting this position is difficult because it feels like loss. But misunderstanding it is more damaging. Policy built on inflated status misallocates effort. Policy built on defeatism abandons opportunity. Britain's challenge is to act like the country it is, not the one it remembers.

The afterimage of empire lingers long after material power has shifted. Britain's global reach, language, institutions, and networks were once backed by industrial scale and financial dominance. Those foundations eroded over decades. The symbols remained. Memory outlasted capacity. This creates distortion. Expectations are shaped by history rather than reality. Britain continues to speak with confidence formed in a different era. This is not arrogance. It is inertia. National self-image changes slowly. The problem arises when memory substitutes for assessment. When history fills gaps left by diminished power, strategy drifts. Britain risks acting on residual prestige rather than present capability. The afterimage flatters and misleads. It obscures limits. Letting go of it does not mean rejecting history. It means updating it.

Britain retains influence, but lacks scale. It has diplomatic reach, experienced civil servants, and respected institutions. It can convene. It can advise. It can shape discussions. What it cannot do consistently is enforce outcomes alone. Economic weight matters. Industrial capacity matters. Market size matters. Britain's leverage is thinner than its presence suggests. Influence without scale relies on cooperation and goodwill. It is contingent. This is not weakness. It is a different mode of power. The danger lies in confusing influence with control. Britain can be heard. It cannot always be decisive. Recognising this distinction allows smarter engagement. Ignoring it leads to frustration and overextension. Influence works best when paired with restraint.

Security is an area where Britain retains credibility. Defence capability, intelligence networks, and alliances provide real weight. Britain remains a serious security actor. This creates an imbalance. Military credibility outpaces economic strength. The country can project force and gather intelligence more effectively than it can sustain industrial or economic leadership. This asymmetry shapes foreign policy. Security commitments feel natural. Economic commitments feel strained. The risk is relying too heavily on security identity to compensate for economic weakness. Power built on force without matching economic resilience is brittle. It invites overreach. Britain must align its security role with its economic base. Otherwise, commitments accumulate faster than capacity.

Trade is discussed as aspiration rather than leverage. Britain speaks of global trade opportunities as if access alone guarantees advantage. In reality, trade terms reflect bargaining power. Market size matters. Supply chains matter. Britain negotiates from a position of limited leverage. This does not preclude beneficial agreements. It does limit their scope. Trade cannot replace domestic capacity. It complements it. Britain often treats trade deals as symbolic victories rather than economic tools. This inflates expectations. When outcomes disappoint, frustration grows. Trade strategy must be grounded in realism about bargaining position. Overstatement damages credibility. Understatement wastes opportunity. Balance is required. Britain has struggled to find it.

Soft power remains valuable, but insufficient on its own. Culture, education, language, and reputation open doors. They create goodwill. They do not compel action. Soft power works best when underpinned by material strength. Britain's soft power persists partly because of history. It will erode if not supported by performance. Reputation depends on delivery. When promises outstrip outcomes, trust fades. Soft power is not a substitute for capacity. It is an amplifier. Britain risks treating it as a replacement. This confuses influence with durability. Culture attracts attention. Capability sustains it. Without renewal, soft power becomes an echo.

Britain's alliances provide strength and constraint. Cooperation with larger blocs amplifies influence. It also limits autonomy. This is the trade-off of being a mid-sized power. Independence rhetoric obscures this reality. Britain can choose partners. It cannot escape interdependence. Alliance dependence is not failure. It is structural. Successful countries manage it openly. They align ambition with alliance roles. Britain sometimes resists this clarity. It seeks autonomy without scale. This creates tension. Accepting constraint allows more effective participation. Denying it produces friction. Real autonomy comes from credible contribution, not rhetoric. Britain must recalibrate its expectations accordingly.

Global competition is harsher than before. Growth is slower. Power is more diffuse. New actors assert themselves. Rules are contested. Britain operates in this environment with fewer advantages than in the past. This is not unique. Many countries face similar constraints. What matters is adaptation. Clinging to old assumptions reduces flexibility. Britain must recognise that room to manoeuvre has narrowed. Choices carry higher opportunity cost. Errors are more expensive. Strategy must be sharper. Nostalgia dulls it. Awareness sharpens it. The global context does not excuse failure. It explains the need for precision.

Overstating status carries cost. It undermines credibility abroad and trust at home. When rhetoric exceeds capacity, partners adjust expectations downward. Citizens become cynical. Britain has experienced this. Promises of global leadership conflict with lived reality. This dissonance weakens authority. Credibility depends on alignment between claim and capability. Honest positioning may feel like retreat. It is not. It is foundation. Countries that understand their position act more effectively. Those that deny it flail. Britain must choose which it wants to be. The cost of overstatement is not humiliation. It is irrelevance through self-deception.

Successful middle powers behave differently. They focus on niches. They build excellence in defined areas. They invest deeply rather than broadly. They coordinate policy tightly. They accept limits and exploit them. Britain has examples to learn from. These countries do not aspire to dominate. They aspire to matter where they can. This requires discipline. It requires saying no to some ambitions. Britain struggles with this. Its history encourages breadth. Its capacity no longer supports it. Adjusting ambition is not surrender. It is strategy. Middle powers that succeed do so by design, not nostalgia.

Realism feels like retreat because it conflicts with identity. Britain's self-image is bound to leadership and independence. Acknowledging constraint challenges that image. Politics reinforces resistance. Leaders fear being accused of decline. This fear produces overstatement. Overstatement produces disappointment. The cycle continues. Realism must be reframed as competence. Accepting limits allows focus. It reduces waste. It builds credibility. Britain must separate pride from policy. Pride preserved through denial erodes faster than pride grounded in honesty. Realism is not pessimism. It is preparation.

Britain can still matter in the world. It can contribute meaningfully to security, diplomacy, science, culture, and problem-solving. Doing so requires acting within limits rather than denying them. Influence will be situational, not universal. Leadership will be collaborative, not commanding. This is not a lesser role. It is a different one. Relearning how to matter requires recalibration, not withdrawal. Britain's future influence depends on alignment between ambition and capacity. The country does not need to be what it was. It needs to be what it is, clearly and deliberately.

Chapter 27 The Generation That Loses Patience

Under-40s report significantly lower trust in political institutions than older cohorts.

This is not a mood swing or a cultural phase. It is a structural fault line forming across generations. Younger cohorts are not merely dissatisfied; they are encountering a system that no longer delivers what it promised. The frustration is cumulative, built over years of unmet expectations. It is not driven by impatience, but by endurance. People tolerate decline quietly until they don't. Britain's younger generations have absorbed rising costs, weaker security, and shrinking opportunity without a corresponding adjustment in rhetoric or policy. The system continues to speak in the language of progress while delivering contraction. This mismatch creates tension. When frustration is dismissed as attitude, the underlying cause remains untouched. The generational divide is not about values. It is about outcomes. That is why it matters.

Younger cohorts experience decline differently because they lack a reference point for abundance. Older generations remember expansion, rising living standards, and widening opportunity. Decline feels relative. For those without that memory, stagnation feels absolute. There is no baseline of progress to retreat from. Life begins constrained. Costs are high from the outset. Housing is inaccessible. Security is conditional. The ladder appears intact but is harder to climb.

This shapes outlook. Frustration is not nostalgia-driven. It is present-tense. Younger generations are told conditions will improve with time. Time has not delivered. The patience expected of them assumes a future resembling the past. That assumption no longer holds. Without visible improvement, trust weakens.

Promises were made implicitly and explicitly. Education was presented as the route to security. Work was framed as the path to stability. Housing was assumed to follow effort. Retirement security was taken for granted. These pathways no longer align. Education often leads to debt rather than opportunity. Work delivers income without security. Housing remains out of reach. Pensions feel distant and uncertain. The system still describes these paths as viable. Experience contradicts it. This creates dissonance. Younger people did not misunderstand the deal. The deal changed. When pathways collapse without acknowledgement, resentment grows. The issue is not entitlement. It is expectation grounded in decades of precedent. When precedent fails silently, legitimacy erodes.

The effort–reward bargain has weakened. Hard work no longer guarantees progress. Many work longer hours for diminishing returns. Productivity gains do not translate into wages. Advancement is slower. Stability is fragile. This is not universal, but it is widespread enough to shape perception. The narrative of effort leading to reward persists. Reality undermines it. This disconnect is corrosive. It discourages investment in the system. When effort is decoupled from outcome, motivation shifts. People disengage or adapt defensively. Trust in institutions fades. The bargain that underpinned social cohesion frays. Britain continues to rely on a moral economy that no longer functions reliably. Younger generations experience this gap daily.

Asset inflation locks out new entrants. Housing wealth accumulates for those who already own. Prices rise faster than incomes. Entry becomes harder each year. This creates a divide not just between rich and poor, but between owners and non-owners. Wealth becomes inherited rather than earned. Younger generations confront a closed system. The promise that ownership follows effort no longer holds. This shapes life choices profoundly. Family formation is delayed. Mobility stalls. Inequality hardens. The system continues to celebrate ownership as normal. For many, it is unattainable. This exclusion is structural, not behavioural. Blaming attitudes misses the point. Asset inflation redistributes opportunity backward. Younger generations see this clearly.

Risk has increased without corresponding upside. Younger people face volatile employment, insecure contracts, and rising living costs. They carry more risk individually. At the same time, accumulation is harder. Savings are thin. Assets are inaccessible. Buffers are weak. The system shifts risk downward while protecting incumbents. This asymmetry matters. Risk is tolerable when it offers reward. Without reward, it becomes destabilising. Younger generations are asked to be flexible without gaining security. This breeds caution rather than dynamism. Entrepreneurship declines. Mobility slows. Risk without upside erodes belief in the system's fairness. Britain's economy increasingly relies on those least able to absorb volatility absorbing it anyway.

Political legitimacy strains when outcomes diverge from promises. Systems maintain authority when they deliver or adapt honestly. When they do neither, belief weakens.

Younger generations vote less or differently. They disengage or radicalise. This is often framed as apathy or extremism. It is better understood as scepticism. Institutions that no longer work as advertised lose credibility. Britain's political language remains optimistic. Experience contradicts it. This gap widens generationally. Legitimacy is not inherited. It is renewed through performance. When performance falters persistently, authority decays. This decay is gradual until it accelerates. Younger generations are closer to that edge.

Patience often runs out suddenly. Long periods of tolerance create the illusion of acceptance. In reality, frustration accumulates. A trigger exposes it. This can be economic, political, or symbolic. The speed surprises those in power. They misread quiet endurance as consent. Younger generations adapt individually until adaptation fails. Then reaction is collective. This pattern repeats historically. Britain is not immune. The warning signs are visible: declining trust, rising cynicism, exit through emigration or withdrawal. These are not dramatic yet. They are preparatory. When belief breaks, it does so quickly. Patience is not infinite. It is conditional.

Frustration expresses itself in many forms. Some disengage entirely. They withdraw from politics, institutions, and long-term planning. Others protest or support disruptive movements. Some leave the country. Some adapt cynically, focusing on personal survival. These responses are often misinterpreted as moral failure. They are rational adaptations to perceived futility. When systems do not reward participation, participation declines. Britain's response has been to moralise rather than address cause. This deepens alienation. Frustration does not disappear when ignored. It changes form. Understanding these forms matters. They shape the next phase of politics and society.

This is not merely youth politics. Generational strain reshapes the entire system. When younger cohorts lose faith, institutions lose future legitimacy. Policies designed for older voters dominate. Intergenerational imbalance deepens. The social contract fractures. Britain risks entrenching a politics of preservation over renewal. This affects everyone. Older generations depend on younger ones to sustain systems. When belief breaks, sustainability falters. The issue is not youth preference. It is system continuity. Generational patience underpins stability. When it erodes, everything built on it becomes fragile. Britain's challenge is systemic, not demographic.

Dismissing generational frustration is dangerous. Labelling it entitlement or impatience avoids responsibility. It misreads signal as noise. History shows that generational disillusionment precedes major change. Sometimes reform follows. Sometimes disruption does. Britain's institutions tend to react late. By the time frustration is undeniable, options are narrower. The cost of dismissal is not just resentment. It is lost opportunity for managed adjustment. Listening early allows adaptation. Ignoring it invites rupture. Younger generations are not asking for perfection. They are asking for plausibility. When even that is denied, belief collapses.

When belief finally breaks, rebuilding it is difficult. Legitimacy lost is not easily restored. Trust requires consistency and delivery over time. Britain still has a window to act. Generational patience is strained but not exhausted. Adjustment can still be managed. This requires honesty about limits, redistribution of risk, and visible effort to realign reward with contribution. If this does not happen, the system will continue to rely on patience that no longer exists. The generation that loses patience defines what comes next. Britain must decide whether that next phase is renewal or rupture.

Chapter 28 After the Pretending Ends

.....

Pretending rarely ends with drama. There is no single moment when denial collapses. It fades. The language changes first. Certainty weakens. Promises become conditional. Expectations quietly adjust. Britain is closer to this moment than it admits. The rituals of optimism continue, but belief thins. People act differently before they speak differently. They save where they once spent. They hedge where they once trusted. They plan shorter horizons. Pretending ends not when leaders confess failure, but when everyday behaviour no longer aligns with official story. This is the real turning point. It arrives quietly. By the time it is acknowledged publicly, it has already happened privately. Britain is approaching that point. The question is not whether pretending will end. It is whether anything coherent replaces it.

Once rhetoric is stripped away, Britain appears neither broken nor triumphant. It is a mid-sized, ageing economy with strong institutions under strain, uneven productivity, and limited fiscal room. It remains safe, orderly, and capable in many domains. It is also slower, poorer relative to peers, and more constrained than it claims. This reality is manageable if acknowledged. It becomes corrosive when denied. Britain still functions because expectations have adjusted without being named. The danger lies in the gap between description and experience. A country cannot plan honestly if it misstates its condition. Removing exaggeration does not diminish Britain. It clarifies it. Acting from clarity allows proportionate ambition. Acting from illusion produces drift.

Honesty feels harsher than decline because it removes comfort. Decline can be endured silently. Naming it demands response. Britain has tolerated deterioration by avoiding language that would force decision. This avoidance feels kinder. It is not. It prolongs uncertainty. It shifts burden onto individuals. Honesty would provoke discomfort and resistance. It would also allow design. Pretending preserves peace at the cost of coherence. When limits are unnamed, trade-offs are hidden. Decisions still happen, but badly. Honesty concentrates pain briefly to reduce it later. Britain has chosen the opposite. This choice explains much of the frustration it experiences. The aversion to honesty is emotional, not practical.

Living in contradiction imposes costs. Institutions lose credibility when outcomes diverge from promises. Public trust erodes. Professional goodwill is consumed. People stop believing what they are told and start acting defensively. This is not collapse. It is hollowing. Britain has maintained form while substance thins. Contradiction demands constant explanation. Explanations exhaust everyone. Eventually, silence replaces defence. The cost of pretending is cumulative. It weakens legitimacy without triggering reform. This is the most dangerous state for a country: stable enough to avoid crisis, dishonest enough to avoid correction. Contradiction drains energy that could be used to adapt. It is not neutral. It is corrosive.

Britain has already lost things. It has lost the expectation that each generation will do better than the last. It has lost ease of mobility. It has lost spare capacity. It has lost the assumption that growth will solve problems automatically. It has lost credibility in some domains through overstatement. Acknowledging loss is not indulgent. It is necessary. Loss shapes constraints. Denying it invites repetition of failure. Britain often behaves as if losses are temporary interruptions rather than structural changes. This misreading fuels disappointment. Accepting loss does not mean accepting decline as destiny. It means starting from where you are, not where you wish you were.

Britain still has real strengths. Institutions endure. Law functions. The state retains competence in key areas. Education and research remain strong. Cultural influence persists. Social order holds. These are not symbolic assets. They matter materially. They provide foundation. Britain is not starting from ruin. It is starting from constraint. Strengths must be matched to ambition carefully. Overstretch weakens them. Underuse wastes them. The danger lies in mistaking residual strength for unlimited capacity. The opportunity lies in deploying strength deliberately. Britain can still choose coherence over spectacle. Its remaining assets make that possible if they are not squandered through denial.

Adjustment is not surrender. It is design under constraint. Surrender abandons agency. Adjustment exercises it realistically. Britain has conflated the two. Any acceptance of limit is framed as retreat. This framing blocks adaptation. Countries that adjust early preserve more autonomy than those forced to adjust later. Adjustment can stabilise living standards, restore trust, and align institutions with reality. It requires saying no to some aspirations to protect others. This is not weakness. It is prioritisation. Britain's difficulty lies not in lack of options, but in refusal to choose among them openly. Adjustment delayed becomes surrender by default. Adjustment chosen remains control.

No rescue narrative is coming. There will be no sudden growth boom, no external saviour, no painless reset. Waiting for rescue has become a habit. It postpones responsibility. Britain has repeatedly delayed adjustment in anticipation of better conditions. This has not worked. Conditions rarely improve on their own. They respond to design. Abandoning rescue narratives is psychologically difficult. They provide hope without obligation. Letting them go feels bleak. It is not. It is clarifying. When rescue is abandoned, agency returns. Britain does not need salvation. It needs alignment. That requires action rather than waiting.

If nothing changes, Britain will become a country defined by managed diminishment. Life will remain orderly but narrower. Opportunity will concentrate. Inequality will harden. Politics will grow more performative. Trust will continue to thin. This trajectory is not catastrophic. It is quietly corrosive. It produces a society that functions but does not inspire. Over time, even stability becomes fragile. This is the default path. It requires no decision. It emerges naturally from avoidance. Understanding this matters. Drift is not neutral. It is a choice made by not choosing otherwise.

Britain could still choose a different shape. Not revival, but coherence. A country that aligns promises with capacity. That defines what it will do well and what it will not. That distributes adjustment fairly. That rebuilds legitimacy through honesty rather than optimism. This alternative is constrained but credible. It does not depend on growth miracles. It depends on design, consent, and discipline. Such a country would feel less grand and more stable. It would trade illusion for trust. This choice remains available, but not indefinitely. Windows close quietly.

Responsibility now lies less with individual leaders and more with systems and consent. Expecting politicians to resolve structural contradictions alone is unrealistic. The public must accept trade-offs. Institutions must be redesigned to sustain continuity. Media must tolerate complexity. Responsibility is collective. Pretending allows everyone to avoid it. Ending pretending redistributes it. This is uncomfortable. It is also necessary. Without shared responsibility, reform collapses. Britain's future depends on whether responsibility is accepted or deferred again.

After the pretending ends, Britain faces a simple question with no easy answer. Not how to restore what was lost, but how to live honestly with what remains. The answer will not be heroic. It will be practical. It will be shaped by limits rather than dreams. That does not make it small. It makes it real. The end of pretending is not the end of Britain. It is the end of one story about it. What follows depends on whether honesty becomes the foundation for renewal, or merely another phase of drift.

www.ingramcontent.com/pod-product-compliance
Lightning Source LLC
LaVergne TN
LVHW090409210926
848480LV00002B/509

* 9 7 9 8 2 3 3 3 1 0 6 5 2 *